Get Up, Dress Up, Show Up

Lessons in Love and Surmounting Grief

by

Petal Ashmole Winstanley

Grosvenor House
Publishing Limited

The right of Petal Ashmole Winstanley to be identified as the author of
this work has been asserted in accordance with Section 78
of the Copyright, Designs and Patents Act 1988

The book cover is copyright to Petal Ashmole Winstanley
Cover photograph by Lynne Wake

This book is published by
Grosvenor House Publishing Ltd
Link House
140 The Broadway, Tolworth, Surrey, KT6 7HT.
www.grosvenorhousepublishing.co.uk

A CIP record for this book
is available from the British Library

ISBN 978-1-80381-810-8
eBook ISBN 978-1-80381-811-5

This book is dedicated to Maggie's – a safe haven for me as my world fell apart – and also to Michael, David and Simon. This is for you.

CONTENTS

PART ONE

THE BEGINNING

There was a time when I allowed my pain to consume me. The wreckage of my life was everywhere. As it wore me down, I began to realise the feeling of loss was familiar. It was instilled in me long ago, even before any true loss occurred.

Now, looking back, I wonder how I survived it. Did the darkness simply lift, or was it that sudden shriek of laughter I heard coming out of my mouth that triggered the onset of my recovery? I'm not sure, but yes, I believe that moment of laughter was when I first felt myself coming up for air. It was the laughter that signalled my life was beginning again, after so much loss. And, for one brief moment, I was myself again.

***

Throughout my childhood my mother was in and out of hospital. I was too young to understand that she was unwell; I didn't even try to fathom the cause of her frequent absences. I only knew she wasn't there. I have no recollection of who fed me, but I do remember being alone at three years old. It was at that tender age that I was sent off to the Sacred Heart Preparatory School run by the Catholic Sisters of Mercy. Outside the gate, clad in a way-too-big prickly brown uniform, coddled in my father's arms, I'd cry and cry, begging him not to leave me there. But he always did. The nuns tried their best to pacify me. Nothing worked. My crying continued, and that's how it was every day. Each afternoon the nuns put me to bed in the tiny structure they called the doll's house. Somehow, I always knew when they were coming for me. I hated that doll's house. It was dark with pretend windows, and inside were half-dressed, sad-looking dolls and a horrid smell I can recall to this day. Small as it was, I could stand up in it, and lie down on the little cot. That tells you how tiny I was. So there, stuck in the doll's house, I was told to go to sleep. But I don't remember sleeping in there, not ever. I was too scared. I just wanted my mother.

At home at last, two things lightened my worries. One was Beauty, my beautiful Collie dog; the other was dancing, which I loved most of all. Whenever I wanted to escape, I'd brush Beauty's ears, clean her paws, and then off I'd go, dancing and twirling around and around until I was exhausted. Finally, I'd flop back onto my adoring dog, worries gone, at least for a while.

* * *

My parents would frequently recount their delighted surprise when, in their early 40s, they discovered they were with child. My mother claimed I was her menopause baby and the greatest gift she'd ever had. My sister was already 12 years old when I was born, so I was brought up mostly as an only child. I remember my father smiling as he recalled people assuming he was my grandfather. I never regarded my parents as old, and I don't remember ever thinking my situation was unusual.

The house I grew up in was cosy in winter and boiling hot in summer. Nobody had air conditioning back then, and the tin roof made the whole house like an oven. Or so I'm told. The truth is, I don't remember being hot—possibly because I was surrounded by my grandfather's paintings of the sea. He and my grandmother lived in a tiny house at the bottom of a lighthouse, and he painted constantly. In our home his paintings were everywhere: hallways, bedrooms and especially the lounge room. Several others, my father told me, were in a famous place in the city where lots of people could see them, not just me. Some of the paintings were huge – much bigger than I was – and some were smaller. I especially loved the ones of big ships that looked like they might topple over into the angry, deep-blue sea.

One of those paintings scared me because the ship was disappearing into the water almost upside down. I worried a lot about the people in that ship. Did they swim home or what? I wanted to ask my grandfather, but he was dead. And so I pondered: did the people swim to his island and climb up the rocks to his little house? I kept asking what happened to those poor people. My mother said they were probably okay, but how could they be okay when their ship was tipping upside down into the water?

My grandfather, you see, was a lighthouse keeper. He loved lighting the huge lamp so the ships with their billowing sails could find their way in the dark. The lighthouse in which he and my grandmother lived was on Breaksea Island—far out on the ocean in King George Sound, off the coast of Western Australia. No one else lived on the island at that time; only the lighthouse keeper and his wife. My mother told me it was a windy place, sometimes so windy that my grandparents had no food because the sea was angry and refused to allow the little boats bearing goods to reach them. They must have been so hungry. I've seen pictures of their tiny house at the bottom of the lighthouse. When I was very young, I loved imagining my grandparents listening for the foghorn from the clippers, those sailing ships that would prompt my grandfather to climb all those stairs to the top of his lighthouse. They had moved from that lighthouse to one on Rottnest Island, which is also in Western Australia and situated 12 miles off the coast of Fremantle. I could never understand why they moved. But I do know that my grandmother loved Rottnest Island, and so did my father, who grew up there until he was six. He didn't like school, he told me, but he loved making little boats that could actually float, collecting shells, finding crabs and playing by himself beside the rock pools. Rottnest Island had lots of small, rat-like mammals called quokkas, which my father used to try and catch. There was also a big stone building where Aboriginal people were kept. My father said they had to stay there forever. I was spellbound, imagining those Aboriginal people sad, crying, hungry. I wondered why they were there—what had they done? Were they orphans who had no mother or father to help them? My parents would tell me to stop worrying, though I kept thinking about it and wondering why nobody cared about those poor people in that place.

Something else that troubled me was why the lady who lived next door to us often had tears in her eyes. I asked my mother what it was that made her so sad. She told me that some angry people had sent her family away in a train, and she never saw them again. "How come?" I asked. "Did they do something terrible or what?"

"It was all a long time ago," my mother replied, "Get along now."

She often told me to "get along", usually when my questioning exhausted her. But I persisted, saying, "But why were they sent away? It's just not fair!"

My mother replied sharply, saying, "Who on earth put the idea into your head that life was going to be fair?"

Her tone told me it was time to back down. But later I would learn of the Holocaust, and then I understood the reason our neighbours' family was sent away on a train.

As I think back over my childhood it's clear to me, as it must be to you, that I was a very anxious child. My parents had to have been relieved when I took to the joys of dancing. Once that happened, I remember my mother often saying, "You're just like your grandfather." I'm honestly not sure what she was implying, though possibly she likened my passion for dancing to my grandfather's compulsion to paint.

* * *

By the time I was 14 my talent for ballet was obvious. Blessed with a well-proportioned body, nicely shaped legs and ballet insteps I was set up to dance. Luckily for me, a ballet school had been established in my hometown of Perth, under the stern guidance of Madam Kira Bousloff. I was one of the strong, dedicated young hopefuls who became her students.

Madam was ahead of her time. Her coaching and care of us was holistic and encouraging, and very different from the autocratic manner I was to encounter in the professional world of ballet. And when this exotic woman captured your heart you could not escape. She was a fascinating figure who spoke French and English with a thick Russian accent. I adored her beautifully arched feet, slender ankles and expressive hands. She demonstrated with precision and style, yet never sought to overshadow her pupils. Despite her vast experience and fame she made sure we, the students, were the stars in the room.

Madam bewildered many citizens of little Perth with her unstoppable, pioneering spirit and ability to influence and intrigue. But for me, as she shared her stories of life in a ballet company, she became even more than my mentor and teacher. She was the person who instilled in me dreams of a world I came to long for. Someday, I promised myself, I will dance in a large and important ballet company just as Madam did years ago.

* * *

When I was 15, auditions were to be held for the newly formed Australian Ballet School based in Melbourne. Successful candidates would enter full-time training there in hopes of earning a place in The Australian Ballet. Madam made it clear that she was not an advocate of the Australian Ballet School training system which, in her view, had adopted a watered-down version of the English Royal Academy of Dance syllabus. Madam taught the Russian Vaganova system, which demanded high levels of technique, energy and passion—aspects of ballet training and performance she regarded as paramount. However, Madam was a professional and a realist who encouraged her students to work toward auditioning for the new school and the opportunity it presented.

Our class in Perth was at fever pitch as the audition drew near. The pressure was on, especially for the top students in the class, of which I was one. My parents were concerned. The fees at the school were extortionate. Train fares, living expenses and accommodation were way beyond their means. Though I knew this, I desperately wanted to be accepted into the school. Being invited to go to Melbourne and train would be a significant step in the right direction. Yet, at the same time, my mother's fragile state physically and mentally left me torn. I had become adept at judging her degree of depression. I had learned how to jolly her along. Sometimes she'd fall beyond the reach of coaxing, at which point I'd dance for her. I'd whizz around our tiny lounge room changing record after record as ballet music blared out on our radiogram. Usually this helped.

She depended on me. I brought light to her world. But if all my tricks failed there would be little I could do other than listen to her. In return, she would read to me from a book by a lady named May Gibbs that was called *The Complete Adventures of Snugglepot and Cuddlepie*. As she read those enticing words to me the stories came to life, leaping out at me, fuelling my imagination, providing me with vivid thoughts and images I would tap into years later when choreographing a ballet inspired by that same book for The Australian Ballet.

When she was free from depression her entire being changed. She was engaging, quick-witted and sharp to catch on to anything unforeseen. Early on, she instilled in me an awareness of style; her wedding dress was certainly a fine example of her elegant taste and appreciation of beauty. She liked to echo a catchphrase of Coco Chanel. "Do not over dress yourself," she'd say. "Before you leave the house take one thing OFF." It was an admonition for which, in later years, I had a few cheeky responses! She insisted I take elocution lessons at school and make the most of myself—meaning lipstick and hair sorted before chores! She was an avid reader and loved teaching me the poems of Henry Wadsworth Longfellow. "The Wreck of The Hesperus" is one I can recite perfectly to this day. Classical music was deeply embedded in her heart, along with works of the artist Thomas Gainsborough, to whom she introduced me at a young age. Above all, and most importantly, she adored me, and I knew it.

And yet, there were times when my mother's mood turned dark, and she would confide in me "I want to sail away and never come back." Her threats of leaving haunted me, creeping into my head and lodging there until I was so full of the fear of loss and abandonment that I couldn't stand it. I'd run out the door to my ballet class or practise my ballet barre on the front veranda, the coolest place in the house: shaded, as it was, by huge gumtrees that lined our street. At other times, my mother actually did need to leave for weeks of treatment at the hospital and I would pack her bag. Knowing she'd be gone for a long time, I'd hide my tears from her. I hated the thought of being without her.

Often when I needed soothing it was my father I would run to. I adored him, as did my mother, and he loved us dearly. He was the sweetest, kindest man. I especially loved his whimsical sense of humour and the twinkle in his eye. Sadly, he was prone to getting tipsy, which upset my mother who'd grown up in an alcoholic household. The chaos she'd witnessed as a child affected her so profoundly that she never took a single sip of alcohol and had little patience for anyone who was even slightly inebriated, which made my father's drinking a constant source of tension. So, ultimately, my haven was the ballet studio where I could dance for hours. And escape.

* * *

I was good at ballet. I loved the feeling I'd get when the music started and off we'd go, legs on fire. People who saw me dance were convinced I had a wonderful future in ballet, and Madam's evident belief in me gave me faith in myself. My mother fervently acknowledged my passion to become a ballet dancer. She would have none of it when the rest of our family insisted that, while ballet is a lovely hobby, I should do something I could fall back on... like nursing! "Take no notice," she would whisper, "be a ballerina."

The audition came and went. I'd done well. Each day, with feelings of anticipation and excitement, I looked forward to a letter of acceptance. As letters began arriving two of my friends were given places. Everyone at our school was thrilled for them. Finally, my letter came. It stated that I was not suitable for the school. I was broken-hearted. I'd been excluded from an important opportunity to pursue what I loved most in the world. After all the hype that had surrounded my ability, I'd simply not matched up. I was plagued by the horrible feeling of shame. I cried a lot, sobbing at night to my mother. I was hurting and nothing could ease my tears. My mother was alternately comforting and furious at my rejection. But Madam saw things differently. She knew my exuberance and buoyant personality would not fit into The Australian Ballet School, with its English style of training. She had always encouraged my fearlessness, and loved the fact that there was nothing I would not attempt. As far as she was concerned, I was a racehorse who would resist being reined in. She knew I was single-minded, impatient and ambitious and – with my above-average technique – she was convinced it would be better for me to go elsewhere.

I appreciated Madam's perceptions of me, yet accepting that my friends were heading off to Melbourne was tough. Once again, I found myself crying a lot and, like the rest of my family, I kept questioning *why not me*? After all, we'd been led to believe I had the potential to become a professional ballet dancer. My mother, who'd never doubted my ability or passion, wrote to the director of the school in Melbourne, demanding a reason as to why I'd not been offered a place. I never saw the director's reply, but I understand it was curt. My mother was enraged. Clearly, I'd simply been cast aside.

In the coming weeks, I attended send-off parties for the chosen few who had landed a place at the school—occasions that were followed by sad farewells as they left by train from Perth to Melbourne. As I bade my friends goodbye, I realised that my future was up to me. I would need to go back to class with Madam and work as hard and well as I could. And that is what I did.

* * *

Sixteen months later, The Australian Ballet arrived in Perth to perform. These dancers were like gods to me. Though images of the wonderful dancers of The Royal Ballet had lined my bedroom wall since I was a child, it was thoughts of the Australian dancers that had inspired me and pushed me to pursue my dream. So it was thrilling that their presence in Perth offered an opportunity to take class with them, as it was usual to allow the top local students to join in classes with the company as a goodwill gesture. I eagerly attended every class I could, showing my best, all the while telling myself that these recent months of training had made me a better dancer, so perhaps I would be noticed and could land a professional contract with the company. But no offer was forthcoming. Rejected again.

There were no other choices for professional ballet dancers in Australia at that time; at least none that interested me. My first real challenge was right there in front of me. What was I going to do?

Then, suddenly, I knew. I would go to London where real ballet happened! That was it... in my mind I was already there. My mother thought this was a great idea. My father was doubtful, perceiving my plan as some fanciful dream I'd cobbled up. Firstly, he reminded me, I'd just turned 17 and would need his permission to leave Australia. Secondly, he was convinced it was dangerous for me to go to London alone, and the rest of our family agreed.

They asked, "Who on earth would want to go to London and starve in a cold attic?"

"I would," I said.

Thinking he'd quash the idea good and proper, my father stipulated that I could go to London providing I'd turned 18, paid my own way and left a return fare with him. I jumped at the challenge and started my plan. Madam employed me as her teaching assistant, working with the youngest students after school hours during the week. On Fridays I'd accompany her, travelling by bus, to country ballet schools. I loved this; not only was I learning the fundamentals of teaching ballet, but I was also getting to spend hours alone with Madam. Our journeys to and from our destinations would end all too soon for me as I'd be engrossed in Madam's stories of travelling by train across Europe when she danced in the legendary Colonel de Basil's Ballets Russe de Monte-Carlo.

Soon, I opened a small ballet school in my local church hall, where I taught on Saturdays with my mother playing the same three pieces on the piano over and over again. My pennies were mounting and, with the added help of a small local benefit performance put on by Madam, I was able not only to pay my fare to London by ship, but also to amass the return fare for my father plus £100 in spending money. I remember the day I purchased my tourist-class ticket for the ship from an agent on Wellington Street in Perth. That ticket was precious and, after proudly showing it to my parents, I hid it under my mattress. I had put aside the disappointment of being rejected by The Australian Ballet School and Ballet Company. I was on a mission. I was happy and full of hope.

As I look back, I can appreciate how brave and generous my mother was in pushing me out of the nest even though she depended on me in so many ways. I suspect she sensed that I was already a grown up. Having been her caretaker for so many years, I'd learned to take care of myself and acquired the ability to read people accurately. And she surely knew I had an irrepressible passion to dance, and buckets of determination to succeed. Her belief in me never wavered, not ever. As for my own state of mind, I truly wonder how I found such blind faith in myself. All I remember feeling was I needed to get away to where real ballet happened! I suppose my fearlessness had been nurtured by my parents and by Madam, the other significant adult in my life. Having joined her school at the age of ten, I'd remained in her care until I left for London eight years later.

* * *

I turned 18 on the 14th of October 1965. Six days after that, the newest flagship of the P&O shipping company, the SS Canberra, berthed in Fremantle en route to London. The ship would stop at Cairo, then go through the Suez Canal as it headed for Naples, before finally docking in Tilbury. I was on board. My family stood on the wharf waving as the huge ship nudged her way from the siding and slowly moved out toward the Fremantle heads and the open seas. Excited as I was to be heading for my new life, the memory of my six-year-old niece Carina waving goodbye is one that I knew would stay lodged in my mind.

The Canberra was a modern, floating '60s beauty. Even below water level, in tourist class where I was travelling, she was bright and shiny, with trendy orange, brown and turquoise décor. I loved being on board this beautiful liner in the middle of the ocean where there was no beginning and no end: just distance. I shared a teeny, tiny cabin in the ship's bowels with three Australians who, although much older than myself, turned out to be good fun. I learned immediately that it was essential to be well organised as there was no space, so our suitcases were held in the belly of the ship with access on certain days at allocated times. The cramped quarters turned out to be good preparation for what would become a lifetime of shared theatre dressing rooms, in which four or five dancers were jammed in together.

Life on board the Canberra was exciting and fuelled my curiosity for the unknown. People were shocked that I was travelling alone and were eager to take me under their wing. The ship had a discotheque with a huge mirror ball and flickering red and green lights. Beatles songs blared out day and night, a harbinger of the swinging London scene I could hardly wait to be a part of. A Paul McCartney lookalike – angel faced, with long floppy hair and a thick Durham accent – caught my eye as we danced each night to The Beatles' "Love Me Do". I do not recall a single moment when I looked back or feared the unknown.

As the Canberra rocked and rolled her way through the sea, my days were spent finding spaces away from staring eyes where I could work on my ballet barre. Keeping in shape concerned me. I needed to be in good condition on arrival in London in order to audition for jobs. Exactly how I would arrange those auditions I had no idea. However, I solidly believed there would be room for me somewhere in that big ballet world.

When I couldn't find the space I needed, I decided to chat up one of the cabin stewards who, with a twinkle in his eye, ushered me to a dead-end passageway: a good-enough narrow spot in which I could practise. Fortunately, ship's passageways are lined with handrails, which acted brilliantly as my barre. I was grateful for the steward's help and didn't mind one bit when he'd pop by to watch me for a few moments as I stood at the barre, working my pliés and tendus.

By the time the Canberra berthed in Tilbury on a cold, foggy morning I had found a new onboard family. I knew I would miss them. Promises of keeping in touch were made, along with exchanges of photographs and addresses, though we never did make contact again.

* * *

In Tilbury, I trundled into a large shed lined with suitcases, hundreds of them. Finally, I found mine. Then I looked around and discovered that my new onboard family had disappeared. I needed to find transport that would get me to Earl's Court in West London. Somehow, I located a friendly official who guided me to a bus. I thanked him and jumped on board. I was on my way. I had to start somewhere, and a bus ride into swinging London was just the ticket I needed.

On a piece of paper in my small, '60s shoulder bag I had three addresses: one for the Overseas Visitors Club in Earl's Court where I hoped to get a room; another for a ballet teacher recommended by a principal dancer in The Australian Ballet; and the third for Max Rivers Studios in Leicester Square where, I'd been told, out-of-work dancers took classes and watched the noticeboard for jobs.

On arriving at the Overseas Visitors Club, I found my way to the noticeboard and picked out a room I could just afford in a huge four-story house that had endless little bedsits and was located not far away, in Tregunter Road. The landlady was gruff as she shuffled me to a rear, windowless room, saying it was available for three nights at three shillings a night. Upon learning I was Australian she haughtily told me that Australians were expensive as they wanted to take daily baths and there was only one bathroom for all the residents. No bath! Even so: I was living the dream!

I paid her, dumped my suitcase, and headed for Piccadilly Circus, passing countless shops and big, beautiful houses, rows and rows of them all joined up, side by side. I don't recall how long that walk took but suddenly there it was, right in front of me: Piccadilly Circus, exactly as the travel pictures had shown. The famed statue of Eros stood proud even in the gloomy autumnal light. The huge, circular Coca Cola sign, the biggest neon sign I'd ever seen, twinkled behind Eros and added to my excitement. I was exactly where I needed to be. I felt welcome. I relished the startling sight of hundreds of people dashing toward the tube, their heads down, protected against the October chill. I wasn't dashing anywhere. All I wanted to do was take in the magic of London, the place where I could fulfil my dreams of becoming a professional ballet dancer, and the place where I would make my home.

The next day I found Max Rivers Studios in Leicester Square. There I was, one of many out-of-work dancers, all of us crammed into a small studio. It was a space that featured pillars placed at odd intervals down the centre of the room; obstacles the London dancers seemed to navigate with ease. They all knew the drill and seemed absolutely sure of themselves, so I followed them, happy to be there though slightly wary of the shouting teacher and the pianist whose eyes darted between the teacher and the dancers. I secretly felt at home being surrounded by like-minded hopefuls. My dancing was good, and I was a natural turner so, once the pirouette section began, I knew I could demonstrate what I was made of. It was good to feel that I belonged.

***

Winter was showing its frosty face that early November. Cold mornings greeted each day. My money was running out. I needed rent, food and cash to pay for classes; in other words, I needed a job. Although I felt confident, I also knew there were many others just as good as me. That was the reality I had to face when I began going to auditions, trying out for cabarets, reviews, West End musicals—anything that seemed even remotely feasible. On each occasion, there would be at least 50 dancers in line outside the audition studio, waiting to be given a number and an audition class time. Though I didn't land a job, each audition consisted of a full, free ballet class, so the upside of this consistent rejection was getting my class for the day free of charge.

Prior to Christmas, the pantomime season was about to kick off. I showed up for countless auditions for Christmas pantos. One afternoon, I went sailing through an audition for a tour of *Aladdin's Lamp*. And I was hired! Contract in hand, I ran to the Piccadilly tube, thrilled to have my first London job. At last: somebody wanted me! And, with my money nearly gone, what a relief to learn that we'd be paid a small per diem for the rehearsal period.

Those rehearsals commenced straight away in Max Rivers Studios, with a morning class given by the very important, very bossy and very scary dance captain. Her class was entirely different from Madam's detailed exercises back home. Things seemed rushed and thrown together, with no room for mistakes or repeats. I was green and inexperienced compared to the other girls, who were seasoned troopers at the panto game. So I had to fit in and pull it together before anyone discovered that the little Aussie from down under was fair game for a good old sending up.

We were scheduled to open in Stoke-on-Trent before Christmas. The other dancers were exchanging information about places to stay so, bluffing away, I managed to get the hang of the "digs" arrangement. One of the dancers handed me a phone number of a Mrs Briggs who ran a boarding house in Stoke where other dancers had stayed before. I called and secured a room for the three-week run of the show. Mrs Briggs was a landlady of few words, among them that I could have two baths a week, and that my room would not be heated. Breakfast would be at 7am sharp and she'd leave a cheese sandwich for me at night. It was all fine with me, except for the fact that I almost froze to death each night, despite going to bed fully clothed to avoid having to strip down in the morning in my freezing room with ice inside the window. It was an experience that left me with a lifelong fear of being cold.

The first show of the day was at 2pm, the second at 7pm. They were lots of fun and it was tremendously exciting to finally be a professional on the stage. The choreography involved a lot of step ball change, skipping and posing; nothing too exacting. I'd get to the theatre early in the morning to work my ballet class and I'd do a ballet barre between shows. I can't remember how much we were paid, but I do recall that I managed to get by on it. By the night of our last curtain call we'd become a close team, and we shed tears and exchanged addresses when saying goodbye.

**

Back in London, I quickly found a room in Earl's Court, which I shared with a fellow Australian who was passing through London as she backpacked her way to France. Our small room was in the basement of a giant terraced house that had been chopped up into bedsits—or rats' nests as they were called. The room consisted of two very narrow single beds, a one-bar electric heater that required one shilling in the metre for an hour of heat, a wash basin and a centre light. With no access to a bathroom this became my first experience of what was known as a "strip wash". It required removing each article of clothing, one at a time, then using a small towel to wash and dry that particular body part, then hurriedly replacing the piece of clothing so your body would never be fully naked in the cold. This was time consuming and made even more awkward because, in the absence of a proper shower or bath, it had to be performed with a mere hand sink. I was startled to learn that strip washing was

17

common in the UK. Gosh, I used to think, these English people are really not keen on bathing. Again, I was cold at night, and the little room was damp, with furry black mould seeping from the ceiling, its stench permeating the room. It was hateful, but I needed to get used to it.

On the noticeboard at Max Rivers Studios, I found an especially enticing audition call: a four-week contract for go-go dancers who would be performing at a new discotheque on the Left Bank in Paris. Four weeks in Paris! Wow. I was there already. The audition was a free-for-all, a do your own thing fest to disco music. In a room jammed full of bopping dancers six of us were chosen. Yippee! I was on my way to France.

* * *

We were taken to Paris by plane, and were all billeted in a large room with a tiny shower wedged in the corner. Breakfast consisted of bread and cheese, which seemed odd to me, and our evening meal would be free at the discotheque. In spite of our excitement on arrival, we decided on an early night, only to be woken the next morning to find one of the girls bitten head-to-toe by bed bugs. Much itching and screaming ensued, causing the landlady to yell at us accusing us of being dirty English people bringing bed bugs to her clean and highly sought-after establishment! Sheets were changed, and smelly powder was sprinkled all over our beds and in our suitcases. We never did find out where the bugs had come from. I did not sleep well during my entire time in Paris.

Our job was to dance on illuminated drums that stood about four feet high and changed colour with each new song. The walls of the disco were carpeted in red, the music was achingly loud, and we girls bopped our hearts out, moving to the pounding beats in crop tops and miniskirts. There were three drums, so we took turns: three dancing, three resting until closing time at 1am. I loved it. What an opportunity to be working in Paris by night, strolling by day along the Seine, visiting markets and – the biggest moment of all – visiting the Palais Garnier, the magnificent opera house where dancers of the Paris Opera Ballet rehearsed and danced. My heart almost exploded as I stood, gazing in wonder at its dazzling opulence, overwhelmed by a rush of longing to realise my dream of dancing in a ballet company. I made up my mind there and then that, on returning to London, I'd rededicate myself to that elusive, fervently desired goal.

* * *

Back in London, I was keen to take daily class. Ballet classes were expensive and a drain on my meagre funds, but they were essential to getting in the kind of shape that would allow me to secure a place in a ballet company. I'd been told about a teacher named Maria Fay, who taught in a basement studio in Philbeach Gardens, West Kensington. She was highly respected and taught at The Royal Ballet School, as well as at other important schools and companies. I managed to find her damp, cold studio and introduced myself to this sunny, energetic, warm woman, who greeted me with affection. Maria always wore a black teaching skirt, black character shoes and pulled her dark hair into a small bun at the nape of her neck. I was drawn in immediately, hanging on her every word. Her inspirational classes proved to be fast, musical and demanding, and were my first real taste of a professional ballet class. At last, I felt like a grown up; no longer a dutiful student. I was finally part of a ballet community. I had found my home. Maria took a real interest in my work, pushing me daily, appreciating my strength— her sharp eye picking up on every detail that needed work.

By now, we were well into the depths of winter. Maria's studio was an old church hall with dark, dank changing rooms located in a disused toilet area in the basement. The floor was sodden, and the air was damp; changing into practice togs was hell, as I was chilled to the bone.

PART TWO

MICHAEL

One afternoon, as I walked down Earl's Court Road, I bumped into Michael Brown, a friend from Perth. We rejoiced like long-lost friends and headed straight to the famous Troubadour Cafe on Old Brompton Road where we talked and talked for hours. He didn't feel like a boyfriend. It was very much like he was part of my sisterhood; he was so like me. It was a time when androgyny was regarded as sexy, and I found his androgenous attitudes and manner extremely attractive. Later I would have a different understanding of what his manner meant.

I'd known Michael when he was at art school in Perth and danced with him in *The King and I* when it came to Perth from Melbourne. I'd always loved his company and quick wit. Michael had been ballet trained. His many talents were a mixed blessing. He was gifted in acting, singing, painting, writing and dancing—an embarrassment of riches that often caused him to meander, unsure of exactly what he wanted to do. His sharp intellect prompted him to ruminate, sometimes endlessly, over his decisions, as he investigated new options and mulled over the best course of action. But he was also delightful company, and it seemed we couldn't get enough of each other. And so, in the heat of a London July, Michael and I decided to get married.

The venue we chose was the Brompton Oratory in Knightsbridge, London—a magnificent, Italian Baroque Catholic Church. I remember going to the priest with Michael and asking to be married in the Oratory, known for its grand occasions, which our tiny wedding would emphatically not be. As it turned out, this priest was great fun, took to us immediately, and granted our request. As I told him, I was a Catholic, so the sole stipulation was that Michael had to agree to a series of Catholic instructions prior to the wedding, which he happily did.

The news that Michael and I were getting married delighted my parents. Ever since my arrival in London I'd sent them rambling weekly letters, colourfully describing Michael and highlighting his sense of fun and his kindness. There was no possibility of them joining us for the wedding: in those days travel by air was expensive, and to embark on a sea journey was something they could no longer manage. So I took the situation in hand and introduced them via letter to Michael's father, with whom they immediately corresponded. Soon they had established a reassuring friendship. Also, since Michael was a Perth lad, it turned out that a friend of his parents lived near to my parents' home—another personal touch that reinforced our relationship. My exuberance and joy were all the confirmation my parents needed to realise that this was a loving relationship, and they gladly gave our marriage their blessing. Although I do not recall a hint of their expressing fear for me, it must have relieved them that I would no longer be alone so far from home.

On the day, I wore a flowered bonnet and kitted out my cream mini wedding dress with white stockings and white ankle strap shoes. The priest had agreed that my mini dress would be acceptable so long as it tipped my knees! Well, in truth, it was way above my knees. I suppose it was mildly scandalous, as it warranted a photo in the evening newspaper with the caption "Bride wears mini dress". I cut the notice out of the paper, and still have it today.

After our service my mother received a letter from our priest in which he told her of our joy and love for each other. My parents were deeply touched. That small act of thoughtfulness meant the world to them; it made them feel included and let them know they mattered and that – even though they had not been present – they were not forgotten.

*　*　*

Looking back, I have no doubt that we were in love, and also part of a vibrant new generation intent on exploring, breaking conventional rules and siding with new-age women who freely spoke out about their rights and needs. The world was changing, and this was a time when women were choosing to leave the confines of housework and homemaking to fulfil their dreams. Skirts became ever shorter and men's hair ever longer. Marijuana and Beatles music sent us floating into hippiedom. Flower power took over... everyone loved everyone, or pretended to.

During the '60s, Earl's Court in London was known as Kangaroo Valley. It was a thriving metropolis of outspoken gung-ho Australians; the tribe from down under had arrived, suntanned and noisy. The English-Australian singing group the Bee Gees bombarded London in the mid-1960s with their falsetto vocals; The Seekers, with their popular folkie love ballads, slinked onto Top of the Pops overnight, hitting number one in the UK, the USA and around the world. Other Aussies included Germaine Greer, feminist, academic, intellectual; when she spoke... we listened! The satirist Barry Humphries taught us to laugh at ourselves; Clive James, journalist, author and critic was known for his quick wit and Aussie straight talk, while Robert Hughes, cultural historian with an encyclopaedic mind, appeared to know everything and more. Mention Australian artists and the names of Sydney Nolan and Arthur Boyd topped the list. And, in the wake of those trailblazers, came Australia's plucky hopefuls: writers, singers, actors, musicians and dancers desperate to have a go.

I'd certainly not travelled from the other side of the world to miss out, so on I stomped with the rest of them. The Brits made fun of our accents, constantly reminding us we were from that place where men are blokes, girls are Sheilas and food is known as tucker. We'd lash back at what we'd call the milky-skinned, floppy, pommy toffs getting their knickers in a twist. The banter caused a ruckus, but none of us took offence.

* * *

The generations that came before us were in shock. Dolly Birds, as we were dubbed, were regarded as bold and disrespectful with far too much to say. They were determined to put us in our place. But that didn't happen... we forged ahead, finding our voice and climbing our way into the work force. Homosexuality had been legalised for those over 21, but there hung in the air a painful prejudice. The Pill was introduced in 1961 for married women only; in 1967 it became widely available, and we all went for it. That same year abortion was legalised up to 28 weeks' gestation.

A new vocabulary entered our common speak: empowerment, visualisation, trendy, flower power, love yourself, enlightenment, love your body, new age, psychedelic, groovy, bread, passion pit, naff, square, do your own thing. As the '70s dawned, we were ready to let go of Mary Quant with her miniskirts and hotpants and Twiggy with her short, pixie-cut hair. We floated into long granny dresses, granny glasses and waist-length hair adorned with flowers. Our bookshelves bulged with self-help books, manuals that – for a brief time – became my bible for reinforcement and clarity.

In the midst of all this, Michael and I were enjoying marital bliss. He had found us a super bedsit attic room on the top floor overlooking Redcliffe Square, Earl's Court. It was in a house that had recently been chopped up into ten modern bedsits. It was fully carpeted, and we had a small kitchen hidden behind a double cupboard that consisted of a tiny Belling cooker and a minuscule fridge and sink. Heating came from a meter on the floor once you put a shilling in the slot, and we shared the bathroom with five other bedsits. There were two public phones on the stairway that rang day and night, alerting anyone passing by to pick up and go knock on the door of whoever the call was for. It may sound primitive, but we were in heaven—loving our little nest above the trees, thankful that we'd secured a home, at least for the time being.

To support our less-than-lavish lifestyle, we got jobs ushering at the ABC cinema on Fulham Road. But, as the weeks passed, our funds were running dangerously low. I explained to my teacher, Maria Fay, that I had to cut back from six classes a week to three. She was concerned, and insisted that in order to secure a job I needed to be in peak condition, and therefore six classes a week were essential. I could not possibly pay for them, so she instructed me to attend her class every day with the understanding that I would repay her once I got a job. Years later, she'd come to Sadler's Wells Theatre to see me dance and wait at the stage door. Each time we met I'd say "Maria, I need to pay you for the classes," and she would reply "Petal darling, you repay me each time I see you dance." I've never forgotten her kindness, and often wonder what might have happened to my career had Maria not been so generous and understanding.

Her example of support and kindness has guided me, and I've tried to pass it on throughout my life.

* * *

Eventually, on the noticeboard at the newly opened Dance Centre in Floral Street, there appeared a notice announcing that a ballet company based in Johannesburg, South Africa was looking for dancers. Both Michael and I passed the audition, signed our contracts and were on our way.

The company, known as PACT – Performing Arts Council of Transvaal – had good studios, adjacent to shady Joubert Park. Our flat was lovely, and not far from Hillbrow, a trendy area where many of the dancers lived. We were welcomed with kindness and curiosity, having flown in from swinging London decked out head-to-toe in Carnaby Street gear.

The director, Faith de Villiers, was well-respected, having taught many of the company's stunning dancers and directed the company with commitment and dedication for a long time. Miss de Villiers was not to be crossed. Her standards were high. She expected each one of us to give nothing less than our absolute best at all times. She was gracious and generous to her dancers, providing frequent, fun-filled braaivleis (barbecues) for the company in the garden surrounding her elegant home. Beautifully turned out, never a hair out of place, she was statuesque and glamourous in her haute couture outfits as she stood on the staircase, checking the conduct and behaviour of her dancers.

I was on a soloist contract; Michael was in the corps de ballet, which suited us both. The repertoire included classic divertissements and an inspirational educational programme for children as well as gems like Balanchine's *Symphony in C* and the lovely, timeless *Giselle* and *Coppélia*. It was exactly what we'd hoped for.

***

South African society provided a learning curve for us. It was a country in the thrall of apartheid, and we found it alarming. As I soon discovered, the word apartheid comes from the language known as Afrikaans, which is spoken by Afrikaners: an ethnic group comprised of South Africa's predominately Dutch, white settlers. Apartheid is their word for "separateness" or "apartness", and its physical manifestations were everywhere. There were separate Bioscopes (cinemas), transport, theatres and public seating that was labelled "nie blankes" (non-whites). We were gobsmacked! And what made it even more horrible was that it had been normalised. In the city, windows were covered with iron bars, some elaborate, some basic and stern. At our friends' homes in the gracious suburbs every door, window and exit was heavily secured and barricaded. I kept thinking, *how on earth could this be*? Not that I was previously unaware of racial cruelty: my father had told me about the Aboriginal people locked in that dank place on Rottnest Island and, as a child, I had worried about the Aboriginals who hung about on the outskirts of Perth, always seeming lost with no place to go. But this was even worse, much worse, and the ill will and disregard shown to Black people made us anxious. Their blatant exclusion was something we found impossible to comprehend.

When we arrived in Johannesburg, Nelson Mandela was in jail; many years would pass before he was released. We felt the disempowerment of Black people. When we questioned why there was no television in South Africa the quick response was some variation of *we don't want to educate the blacks*. Black people had to carry identification, which

27

restricted entry to certain places and areas. White supremacy stared us in the face. One could not escape the grotesqueness of this behaviour.

On a few occasions we attempted to say what we were thinking, but we were instantly shut down. We learned to curb our voices; apartheid was a dangerous subject for us visitors to get caught up in. But the elephant in the room was never far away.

We'd been in Johannesburg only two weeks when Miss de Villiers asked to speak to me in her office. I wasn't sure what to expect. When I arrived, afternoon tea was served by her staff boy in a delicate Minton cup and saucer, after which she quickly got to the point. She wanted me to curb my familiarity with the staff. I was bewildered. What on earth was she talking about? It turned out that I had been seen chatting in a friendly manner to Black members of staff, and that this behaviour was not acceptable and should immediately cease. Nevertheless, I continued to be polite and kind to our staff. There was no way I could bend to such a heartless demand.

I also took care to be kind and polite to the African house boy who came with our apartment and cleaned our flat and washed our clothes. His accommodation was on the roof of our building along with other houseboys. We also had a house cleaning woman whose name was Edna. We got on well and became friends behind closed doors. Edna spoke many African dialects and had eight children. Unlike our houseboy, she had to leave Johannesburg in the late afternoon and travel to a township area outside Joburg where only Black people lived. I had been told by the caretaker of the building not to leave food for the house staff, but I did anyway. Edna knew anything left on the bench in the kitchen in a paper bag was for her to take home if she wanted to. That was our arrangement, and I stuck to it. I'd be dammed if I was going to be told what to do in my own flat.

One afternoon, I arrived home early to find Edna flat on her back on the loungeroom floor, clearly unwell. When I insisted she move onto the sofa she became distressed. With fear in her voice, she explained that if she did what I asked the White caretaker woman who oversaw the building would send an evil, dangerous spirit called the Tokoloshe to get her. No amount of coaxing would convince Edna to get off the floor and onto the sofa. Finally, looking downtrodden, she agreed to go home slightly early. But her fear of doing so was palpable and left me feeling sad.

* * *

As well as performing in Johannesburg, Pretoria and Cape Town we toured the Transvaal jammed into a bus and Combi van, stopping to perform in many little dorps (small towns) and staying in rondawels (small round huts with thatched roofs). We were billeted along the way. One grand home I will never forget was White Water Ranch, which was adjacent to an emerald mine and situated beside a fast-moving river where white elephants had been seen. Sadly, while we were there, no white elephants appeared, but the thought that they might was enchanting. I do recall, however, one of the corps de ballet boys announcing at breakfast that, as he staggered back to his rondawel late at night, he'd caught sight of a large white shadow hovering near the site. It was a good story, though I rather think the local grapes may have accounted for this vision!

We also travelled from Johannesburg to Rhodesia (as it was known then). We were thrilled to be on tour. One afternoon a beautiful giraffe was sighted walking alongside our bus. The driver stopped and the giraffe very gently rested her head against my window. I will never forget her long eyelashes which she used like feathers, dusting her eyes.

We were happy, loving our professional life, living the dream. Everything I did involved Michael's input. It mattered to me that his response to my taste in music and art was always enthusiastic. I valued and relied on his opinions about clothing, make-up and fashion. He sharpened my wit every day, and I had to work hard to keep up with his steel-trap intelligence. We shared an innate emotional connection that I'd never known with any other human being. What I loved most about Michael was his natural, loving, effeminate way, with which I'd identified so deeply and easily. At a time when androgyny still equated with glamour, we had felt no need to define Michael as gay or straight; instead, I regarded him as fluid—an enigma I found deeply attractive.

Our eighteen-month contract came to an end. It was time for us to leave South Africa. We cried when saying farewell to the wonderful friends we made there. We knew we would miss Africa's earthy aroma and dusty, breathtaking landscape. But it is also true that dancing for segregated audiences was astoundingly painful, and we never overcame our sorrow that Black people were not permitted into the theatre to watch us perform. Before a show, the theatre doors would close, keeping us inside while locking Black people out. What a terrible powerlessness we felt as those theatre doors banged shut.

* * *

Arriving back in London, we quickly found a room in Sinclair Road, West Kensington. I had a plan – or should I say a hope – of auditioning for a very fine London-based company, London Festival Ballet. I had friends who danced with the company, and through them I'd already arranged to take company class.

I was well prepared, having accumulated considerable stage experience in South Africa and, having performed a varied repertoire, I felt confident. But I immediately saw that the class was jam packed, allowing very little opportunity to show my ability. I was surrounded by beautiful dancers decked out in the latest 1970s dance wear: leg warmers, plastic pants, tracksuits, different coloured lycra all-overs. Some of the women wore what looked like pink petticoats cut off to just above the knee. I desperately wanted to be part of this company. But at the end of class I was approached by Beryl Grey, a former Royal Ballet principal dancer who was now London Festival Ballet's director. She had observed the last part of the class and briskly told me, in a frosty, autocratic voice that she had no contracts and, furthermore, at a mere five feet in height I was too tiny for her company. I slinked to the side of the studio, embarrassed and deflated. Friends gathered around trying to console me with hugs, cigarettes and words of encouragement, but nothing could appease me. Some of the dancers, seeking to make me feel better, offered a litany of complaints about dancing in the company: they're overworked, the hours are excessive, the repertoire is boring. I'd do better to go elsewhere, they said. I was not comforted: these dancers had what I so dearly wanted.

* * *

In the coming weeks, it seemed that London had lost its glow. The longing I'd had to live there and become part of this wonderful city was diminishing. If I had been hoping for unbridled happiness and exciting opportunities, what I was experiencing instead was a desperate shortage of money and the discomfort of being constantly cold. Wherever I went – houses, flats, shops, theatres – the damp ate into my bones. I was sick to death of baked beans, yoghurt and cottage cheese and was starting to sound like a disgruntled, outspoken Aussie—the kind to whom people say, "Why don't you just go home then?" But giving up and going home to Australia was not an option. I needed to pull myself together and get back on track. Even Michael's wit failed to lift my spirits or boost my energy. Why was it not my turn? I'd have been so useful to London Festival Ballet. Yet Beryl Grey had dismissed me with a wave of her very long arm. At 5'7", which is tall for a ballerina, she had stared down at me so icily. But, I told myself, at her height everyone must seem small!

As the days went by, I was increasingly on edge, impatient and feeling fierce even as I willed myself to be calm. I knew I was in a dangerous state; it was imperative that I stop ruminating on my rejection at London Festival Ballet. No matter what, I thought, I must keep trying.

Michael's father was a darling gentleman who would help us out each weekend with a slap-up meal at Veeraswamy, an Indian restaurant just off Regent Street. We'd meet Poppa, as we called him, outside the Strand Hotel, then walk to the restaurant. Michael and I used to laugh as Poppa, in his sweet way, would ring us the night before and never fail to say "Remember to dress well tomorrow, we'll be walking down the Strand." We loved him dearly.

Michael was adopted as a tiny baby when his much older parents were living in Bombay. At the time, Poppa was director of a large shipping company based there, and it was in Bombay that he had met and married his beautiful Anglo-Indian wife, Ivy. Michael did not know he had been adopted until after Poppa and Ivy had died. Only then did his uncle tell him the truth. He was their only, much adored child who slept with Ivy, his beloved Mama, until he was 15. These were days when couples routinely had separate bedrooms, and Michael never questioned his unusual sleeping arrangement with his mother, although I wondered about her motivation and rationale for encouraging such intimacy. At times I thought that perhaps this explained Michael's ease with women. But I suspected it could be quite damaging—though Michael remembered his youth and upbringing with humour and love. He enjoyed telling me how, at age nine, he would dress up in his mother's clothes and dance for her lady friends after their weekly card game. He also recalled that the headmaster at his school called his father asking what Michael liked to do, as he refused to join in with the other boys or to participate in the sports on offer. His kind father answered honestly, saying Michael loved his art lessons and that his favourite thing to do at home was to pick flowers with his mother, adding that they had the most enormous garden so why wouldn't he want to pick flowers? But this was most definitely not the answer the headmaster of a boys' school wanted to hear. Michael's particular ways caused him and others discomfort, as this was a time in Australia when boys were expected to present as hearty blokes. Inevitably, he was bullied at school, and on his last day there his anger about the ugly treatment he'd received finally surfaced and, when he got home, he gathered up all of his school uniforms, reports and books and marched down to the bottom of the garden where the incinerator for weeds and rubbish was stored and lit fire to the lot.

Michael's mother died when he was 16. Three years later, when we met in Earl's Court, it was obvious to me that he was carrying a terrible load of raw grief. It may well have been that he went directly from his mother's loving arms into mine. If this was the case, Michael chose well. I was good at caretaking, though ultimately I wondered if he perceived me more as a comforter than as a lover. It was something that occasionally nagged at me, and I would come to know the truth, but later.

* * *

Just as my desperation was reaching the point at which it threatened to overtake me, an open audition for a Canadian company appeared on the noticeboard at the rehearsal studios in Floral Street, Covent Garden. Without knowing who the audition was for, Michael and I tottered off to it along with at least a hundred other dancers, all of us hoping to get lucky. The audition consisted, as usual, of a full ballet class; its extreme difficulty left me thinking that the standard of this company must be very high, so it must be a job worth having. It turned out that the audition was for Royal Winnipeg Ballet, the first ballet company to be given a Royal Charter. Michael and I were ecstatic when we were both offered contracts.

***

Winnipeg is situated far north of Manitoba, smack in the middle of the Canadian prairies, where the land is smooth and flat as far as the eye can see. We were due to arrive there in three weeks. We didn't give a second thought to leaving our flat and, since money was so scarce, our London winter coats and boots would have to do (or so we assumed, as we were oblivious to the perils of North America's extreme temperatures that awaited). Fortunately, after our first rehearsal, our flimsy winter gear was noticed by one of the dancers, who escorted us to Portage Ave to kit us out with heavy-duty, long winter coats. As we'd not completed our first week we had no income, and certainly no extra cash. But the company's management realised our fragile economic state and kindly helped us out with an advance salary, which gave us the extra money to purchase that much-needed warm clothing.

Royal Winnipeg Ballet was a small company: just 25 dancers, all of whom were kind and welcoming, as was the artistic director, Arnold Spohr. We quickly found a flat and plunged into rehearsals for a coast-to-coast bus tour of America, during which we would perform in a different city, night after night, for ten weeks. We were under pressure to learn the repertoire and master it. The rehearsal days were long, but I was never tired, as the thought of touring America was all the inspiration I needed to work until I dropped.

It was around this time that we joined a small group of Buddhists, who encouraged us to gather with them for morning chanting sessions. This was quite a fashionable trend at the time, and we both found the practice useful and calming. I added it to my daily practice of yoga, but Michael would fully embrace Buddhism, and later in his life it would bring him comfort when he most needed it.

One of the most memorable experiences I had in Winnipeg was working with Agnes de Mille, a former dancer and gifted choreographer. Her distinctly American, groundbreaking works include *Rodeo* and *Fall River Legend*, which told the story of the murderous Lizzie Borden who, as the children's rhyme goes, "...took an axe and gave her mother forty whacks; When she saw what she had done, she gave her father forty-one." As Agnes set *Fall River Legend* on our company, she opened my mind to the importance of dialogue during rehearsals. She was articulate and humorous and had a fast and fascinating way with words. She declared, with her twinkly smile, that she could not remember my name. Instead, she called me Blossom, which I embraced with amusement. Unlike many choreographers I would encounter later on, she spoke with clarity, and I was able to comprehend precisely what she required of me.

I was cast as Lizzie as a child. This meant that I was present at all coaching rehearsals, listening and learning. My heart was set on performing the role of Lizzie so, hat in hand, I asked Miss de Mille if I could please understudy Lizzie. Hearing my earnest request, her eyes sparkled with affection as she told me it was a good idea for me to learn the role for later on in my career, but that at this stage I was still too

wonderfully young to be cast as Lizzie. Wonderfully young...
I loved that idea! So, off I went, bursting with hope and
thinking *I'll surprise Miss de Mille, I'll handle that age gap no
problem!* In actual fact, I never did get to dance the role of
Lizzie Borden and, looking back at her response to my request,
I can see that it was not only correct but encouraging. One
day, I confessed to her that, compared to American dancers, I
was less flexible and lacked their height of limb. Her reply
was, "Blossom your greatest competition is the dancer you
know you can be. She's the one you need to worry about." It
was brilliant advice, and I have passed it on over the years to
many dancers I've worked with in schools and companies.

* * *

Our biggest surprise would come with the arrival of winter,
when temperatures plummeted. Nothing could have prepared
me for a world blanketed in snow, miles and miles of it,
terminating only when the land met the sky. Unlike London,
Canada had super up-to-date heating systems everywhere; at
last I could stop panicking about being cold! Even so, I was
fearful of frostbite as I trudged off through thigh-high snow,
draped in my black floor-length maxi coat, long black hair
tucked beneath a thick red shawl.

When it came time for our tour to begin, our huge
touring bus surfed its way across that icy white carpet of
snow. There were no trees, no homes, no animal life in sight.
This was a strange, magical realm. Daylight tinged the snow
with a mysterious blue light, disrupted only by sudden bursts
of sunrays as powerful as spotlights on a stage—waking me,
insisting I pay attention and soak in these precious moments.

During the tour, we lived and worked as a close-knit
family, with Mr Spohr and his dedicated ballet staff at the
helm. Our salary was fairly generous and topped up by a good

per diem, which meant we would be able to accumulate a stack of savings. We danced in every state in the USA, travelling by day, lobbing ourselves into yet another Travelodge in the late afternoon, making a quick trot to the nearest food store for after-the-show food, hurrying to the theatre for a warm-up ballet barre, then straight into make-up and costumes and curtain up. Each dancer in the company danced every night for weeks and months on end.

Although Michael enjoyed the repertoire, he especially loved touring the USA and, later on, the world. He became a beloved and popular member of the company; the one to be relied upon to lift the mood on our long bus journeys. He would be in his element mimicking the ballet staff and dancers with his clever wit and dialogue. We all loved his impromptu performances, which came as a blessing during those tours. But ballet was never enough for Michael. His curiosity about so many things would side-track him from focussing on his ballet technique, and he didn't really find the physical aspect of ballet engrossing. His head would scramble with ideas about writing, painting and producing theatre works. This unsettled mind set was often hard to live with, but he held my interest like no other ever did or would.

My own focus on ballet never wavered. Repertoire opportunities constantly came my way as I was quick to learn, had a strong, reliable technique and a voracious appetite for the stage. From the start of the tour, I was thrown into every ballet at a moment's notice, and I quickly realised the benefit of being in a small company. There was no waiting in line for a longed-for opportunity, no waiting for a dancer to leave or become injured in order to score a performance. I was eating up every break that came my way. The pace was gruelling, but I thrived in the knowledge that if I could do this, I could do anything. I worked my way quickly to the top ranks of the company, dancing opening nights throughout Canada and

USA. There were many thrilling moments on stage and off it—
as when Prime Minister Pierre Trudeau and Barbara Streisand
attended one performance, and I was introduced to them
afterwards.

Dancing the difficult *Le Corsaire* pas de deux on opening
night in Toronto, one of Canada's major cities, will stay in
my memory forever. Having rehearsed my fouettés – a
bravura step that came easily to me – somehow, when the
moment came to perform them on stage, I fluffed the entire
sequence. I was devastated, and retreated to my dressing
room, where I could hear Mr Spohr yelling my name. He
arrived in my room furious, demanding to know what had
happened. Breathless, upset and angry with myself I tried to
appease him by reminding him that I'd executed the sequence
perfectly in the studio just days before. This incensed him
even more and he shouted, "I don't pay you $300 a week to
see it in the studio!"

A few performances later, I managed to redeem myself
and all was forgiven.

***

After performing in America, we went onto France and Italy,
and then something amazing occurred: we arrived in
Australia, where I would introduce Michael to my parents
who would, for the first time in five years, see me dance.

In addition to Michael and me, there were two other
Australians in the company. We were welcomed by an
abundance of articles in the press adorned with proudly
nationalistic headlines, among them "Australians Return
Home as International Professionals". To perform in my home
country with a professional company was a massive gift,
allowing me an opportunity to prove to those who'd cast me
aside that I was, after all, a worthwhile dancer.

As a reject of The Australian Ballet School and The Australian Ballet, the euphoria I experienced during our Australian engagements is a feeling I will never forget. One thing I'd come to understand after my Australian disappointments is the truth of a saying I heard along the way, which is another bit of wisdom I've passed on to my students worldwide: "Some come through the door marked enter – and some come through the door marked push." I was a pusher. And I knew in my heart that never again would I be cast aside because, for the rest of my professional life, I would keep on pushing.

My parents were overjoyed to see me on stage doing what I loved. I was repaying them for the anguish and concern they must have felt when I left Australia. Watching me dance with an international ballet company must have been confirmation for my mother that she had been right to push me out of the nest.

While in Melbourne, Michael and I made our first property investment: a tiny two-storey house in what is now a bijou suburb of south Melbourne Garden City. On our first morning, off we walked into an estate agent office armed with our entire savings. The agent, quick to see a sale, presented his selection of available homes. We fell in love with the first one we saw: a little dwelling based on English home design of the 1940s. By the time the company left Melbourne five days later, heading to Sydney, we were proud property owners.

For the next few years, the house was let by the agent, enabling us to gather funds to invest further down the line. Australians of my generation were encouraged to invest as soon as possible in bricks and mortar; this was the thinking my parents had instilled in me. I was wise to heed their advice, and would become quite the savvy property investor throughout my dancing career, during which I enjoyed being a property owner and landlady—an avocation Michael supported wholeheartedly.

* * *

After the Australian and European tours ended, Royal Winnipeg Ballet returned to Canada, where we were booked to amalgamate with a rock group called Lighthouse. The choreographer was a Canadian, Brian McDonald, and the programme was named *Ballet High*—a cannabis-inflected play on words from the Bali Ha'i in the musical *South Pacific. Ballet High* was a new-age, experimental, rock ballet programme. We dancers got right into the groove and vibe. A ballet company on tour with a rock band was a massive change from our structured ballet tours. Suddenly, all of us classical dancers had become cutting-edge rock cool.

During the weeks touring with Lighthouse we played to packed to houses and loved every moment of it. Yet, by then, Michael had become restless and weary of ballet company life. He yearned to explore his other passions: writing, painting and acting. We both knew freelancing might be the answer for him, so he decided to leave the company. I fully supported his decision, knowing that departing the company was also in the offing for me. My plan was to return to London and try once more for London Festival Ballet. With the experience I'd gained in South Africa and with the Royal Winnipeg Ballet, I reasoned, surely Beryl Grey would have to hire me.

When I told Royal Winnipeg Ballet's director, Arnold Spohr, that I would be leaving, he was enraged. He shouted, "I'm gonna make you a North American star! Why would you leave after all this work?" I was grateful for the abundance of performing opportunities Royal Winnipeg

Ballet had given me, but my mind was made up. I had a path to follow, and Michael was eager to enter the uncertain world of freelance work in the hope that one day the right door would open for him. We knew precarious times probably lay ahead for us both, but these were risks we were prepared to take.

* * *

Three years had passed since I'd last set foot in the studios of London Festival Ballet. As determined as ever, there I was once again, auditioning for the company. I was revved up and ready. This time Beryl Grey asked to see a solo. Well prepared, I handed the pianist the sheet music to the Bluebird solo from *The Sleeping Beauty* and the *Giselle* Peasant pas de deux girl's solo, which I must say I felt I knocked off rather brilliantly—only to be told once again that I was not suitable for London Festival Ballet. To make matters worse, Beryl Grey informed me in her cut-glass English accent that – as she'd said before – I was awfully small and simply would not fit beside her line-up of fairies. Holy God. Devastation once again. I was flattened. But then one saving thought occurred to me: I thought back to my father's reply when, as a tiny child, I asked him. "Will these small teeth grow, and will I ever be a big girl?" He replied, "Expensive perfume comes in little bottles." I was perplexed by his answer, but the familiar, loving twinkle in his eyes reassured me that, whatever it meant, it was good.

Nevertheless, in the days that followed, I could not stop castigating myself. Maybe I should have listened to Mr Spohr and stayed in Canada. I even thought maybe I should have done that reliable thing my family members had suggested back in Australia and become a nurse... No! Surely not! But a nagging inner voice kept asking if I had been deluded in thinking there was room for me in the British ballet world.

* * *

I decided to audition for The Royal Ballet. Michael encouraged me, and I figured I may as well take a shot at it. After all, I had nothing to lose. We set about making a list of the positives and negatives for my becoming a member of this beautiful ballet company. Actually, to my surprise, there were quite a few positives: I had a good technique, was quick to learn, at ease on stage and had a varied repertoire behind me; I could turn like a top and knew how to work hard. But the three negatives were serious liabilities: I was 25 years old, a tiny five feet tall and had not trained at The Royal Ballet School. Still, I had to try. I'd been told by dancers that a lady named Iris Law ran The Royal Ballet company, and that I should speak to her.

It was a summer day in 1975 when I trotted along to the company rehearsal site in Talgarth Road, Barons Court and asked where I could find Miss Iris Law. Almost instantly there she was, listening to my request to please allow me to audition for the company. She looked somewhat taken aback, probably because everyone knew in those days that The Royal Ballet had no need to audition outsiders. It was not their policy. Miss Iris Law politely told me that all their dancers came from their school, and that I would therefore not be able to audition. However, I sensed it would be okay for me to push further, so I told her I was familiar with the company policy, but that I was Australian and had come all this way from the other side of the world to join a British ballet company. I had experience and was a good dancer. Good God, what must I have sounded like! I remember feeling that I'd won her over, and in a slightly begrudging way she said I could join the company class the following day. I left feeling exhilarated. Of course, I would have to shine in the class, but I knew how to shine. Maybe, just maybe, it was my turn after all. We had no sleep that night. Instead, Michael coached me in self-belief and kept reminding me to go to the front of the class for the pirouettes. "Grab your moment, Petal," he said.

The next morning, I arrived at the studio and found my way to the dressing room. I immediately got the vibe of the room. Everyone looked to have their spot, so I dumped my stuff in a corner and followed one of the dancers into the Waverley Studio. And there they were: a studio full of exquisite Royal Ballet bodies, all of my dreams right there, doing their pre-class stretches at the barre and on the floor, right in front of me. My eyes darted from Antoinette Sibley to Anthony Dowell to Ann Jenner, Monica Mason, David Wall and David Ashmole. It was as thrilling as it was unsettling, and all I could do was keep telling myself concentrate, concentrate. Halfway through the barre the teacher glided by me and asked, "How old are we?"

"Twenty-five," I told her, but she had not waited for a reply and was gone.

After the class I took myself down to the canteen, where I gazed again at those beautiful creatures—the women decked out in knitted practice clothes in soft feminine colours. They all looked the same: hair immaculate, white teeth, svelte limbs, elegant English accents. I felt a bit like the runt of the litter in the presence of these thoroughbreds. I wondered *do you have to be born beautiful to get into this ballet company?* It sure looked that way to me.

I hung around the studios, mesmerised as I peeked in at rehearsals. Finally, I found Miss Law and begged her, "please, please can I do class tomorrow?" She said I could. Wow! I was on a winner here. And the next day I was told I could come to class again. At the end of that third class, I worked up the nerve to ask if Mr MacMillan, the director of the company, would look at my work. She didn't say yes, but she did say to come in the next day and wear pink tights, not black!

That day, after the barre, in walked the associate director, Peter Wright, and the company's director and much-lauded chief choreographer, Kenneth MacMillan. The tempo of that day's class was fast and furious, but I kept up and knew I'd managed okay. When class ended, Peter Wright waved me to come over to him and Mr MacMillan. He asked, "Are you Petal, and is Petal your real name?"

"Yep," I replied, "that's me!"

They seemed tickled by my answer. Peter Wright then asked me lots of questions: where did I train, who was my teacher, how old was I and did I have residency in the UK? I replied that, due to my English grandparents, I had ancestral residency, and could therefore remain in the UK for as long as I wanted. He then gave me the opportunity I'd been waiting for by asking where I had worked. I couldn't help myself, it all came out in one huge gush: South Africa, Paris disco dancing, Royal Winnipeg Ballet. I followed that with my thoughts on becoming a teacher, even, perhaps, a choreographer one day, and then gave him an endless list of solos and principal roles I'd danced. Every so often, Peter Wright would move close to Kenneth MacMillan and say something to him. I couldn't hear exactly what it was, or what MacMillan replied, though I could see that they were amused by my rant and even encouraging me to continue. I got the impression Kenneth MacMillan was rather shy while Peter Wright was inclined to be chatty and inquisitive. As I'd not attended The Royal Ballet School, I really didn't appreciate the weight these men carried. I galloped on and on and then, finally, amazingly, Peter Wright said they had a position for me on a tour with the educational programme called *Ballet for All*. If I joined the tour, when it ended, they might be able to offer me a coryphée contract. I almost hugged them. I'd cracked it!

* * *

Rehearsals started straightaway. There were eight dancers in the group including the outspoken, ambitious, hilarious Derek Deane, who clicked with me immediately. His wit and sense of the ridiculous was a delight, and we forged a close relationship that has lasted a lifetime. Derek got on with Michael famously; the repartee between them was lightning-fast and hilarious. Life had never been so good. Michael was happy, enjoying writing and painting, dancing part time in the opera ballet performances and delving into Buddhism. And I was working with an interesting group of dancers, performing potted versions of the Royal Ballet repertoire. I knew I was in a try-out situation and did my best to fit in. At the end of the tour, I was thrilled when the coryphée contract Peter Wright had mentioned as a possibility became a reality. I would be dancing with the newly formed Sadler's Wells Royal Ballet, with the proviso that in six months I'd be promoted to soloist. I called my mother reversing the charges. She was ecstatic, asking if I was dancing with Margot Fonteyn, to which I replied I wasn't exactly dancing *with* her but for sure she was there in the ballet class at the back of the room. My darling mother was beside herself with joy, as was I.

I never did have a familiar relationship with Margot, but I was enthralled by her—though not because of her technique or anything in particular about her dancing. It was her unexplainable attractiveness and her ability to entrance an audience; her presence, wherever she happened to be, was riveting. She was the essence of less is more. Her well-proportioned body was designed to dance, and her long neck and classic features defined the ballerina look of that time. She seemed to exude royal elegance, her British charm and gentleness shading the steeliness required to carry out her responsibilities as The Royal Ballet's Prima Ballerina. This she did so magnificently that, in 1979, in tribute to her greatness, she would ascend to the highest possible, rarely given ranking: Prima Ballerina Assoluta.

It was during our performances of *Raymonda* in Athens that I would witness a quality she wasn't known for but possessed in abundance: her brute strength. This was late in her career, and watching her challenge her well-worn body in bravura passages of dance I could only imagine how difficult this must have been for her. Yet, even under duress, her magic was present. I watched carefully, trying to work it out. Was this star quality, X-factor, acting? Or was she simply being her authentic self? I was as fixated on her as I was on Rudolf Nureyev. What was it that made these two stage creatures so intoxicating? Together or individually their distinguished fame and legend have never been repeated. Was it their God-given beauty, talent and sexuality that we found so alluring? I think so... what I know is that we were all hooked.

In my time with *Ballet for All*, rehearsals were held at Barons Court in over-crowded premises that housed The Royal Ballet resident company, the Sadler's Wells Royal Ballet and The Royal Ballet Upper School students. At the side of the building there were a few parking spaces where, if lucky, I could park my car, enjoying a giggle should I manage to slide in beside Rudolf Nureyev's nifty little chocolate brown Fiat sports car. I marvelled at this dancing creature, with his slanted smile and beanie cap worn low on his forehead above his steely eyes. The dance world was in love with him, as was the rest of the world. He was tiger-like on the stage, impossible to ignore as he seduced his audiences.

Rudolf Nureyev had bombarded the dance world— breaking rules, procedures and regulations with his slightly boyish aplomb, supported by massive ability. He could stay in the air longer than any male dancer ever had; he turned more pirouettes and pushed his energy to the limit as he ate up every inch of the stage. He was magnetic, exotic, a creature of wonderment, quick-witted, mischievously rude, sensitive and utterly beguiling. His work ethic was exceptional. He'd practise and rehearse relentlessly, leaving no stone unturned until he was satisfied. I always sensed that, even when his body had reached its daily limit, in his head he was never done. But I knew too about his well-earned reputation for being moody, even irrational at times, so I was also wary.

On one of our Sadler's Wells tours, he joined us in Edinburgh where, it turned out, he did not really remember the choreography for Oberon, the role he was to dance in Frederick Ashton's ballet version of Shakespeare's *A Midsummer Night's Dream*, titled simply *The Dream*. As any friend of Rudolf's knew, when he was stressed he was capable of saying the most vulgar, outlandish things—and towards the end of the ballet, during one of Oberon's fast exits, as I was preparing to enter the stage as a super fairy, he crashed into me and demanded to know where his next entrance was. Distracted, I responded "I don't know."

Glaring at me he said, "Your brain is in your clitoris."

Somehow unphased, I replied, "Gets more use there." Then I turned away from him and headed onto the stage.

From that day on, when our paths crossed, he'd look at me with a wicked twinkle in his eye and a finger pointed directly at me and say, "Ahh you...!" He clearly thought my response was hilarious. I've dined out on that tale ever since!

During the following years, Rudi continued to dance around the world, unable to let go of his love of dance. The last time I saw him was in Australia, shortly before his death. He was unwell and struggling to perform, but the animal was not giving in easily. His powerful presence, raw desire and urgency to keep going were palpable. During a rehearsal at that time, someone took a black and white photograph of him that tells an authentic tale of love. He's sitting on the floor of an Australian Ballet studio, studying the feet in the air of a young male dancer. Although haunted and frail by then, the longing in his eyes reveal that he remembered well how it feels to be suspended above the floor. But instead of regret for times gone by there is a look of pride and pleasure in what he sees, and maybe a hope that he had added to that young dancer's inspiration. To me, it was a look that said *the future of ballet is in your hands and I'm not one bit worried.*

Rudolf Nureyev died in Paris in 1993 at the age of 54. I believe he died knowing that he had changed the world of ballet. The days of men shying away from ballet were done. He had made it acceptable for men to dance, and to express love and passion publicly. He opened the door to freedom for male ballet dancers, allowing them to dance their truth.

* * *

With rehearsals in full flight, I wondered how on earth I was going to learn all of those ballets. Doing my best to fit in, I was thankful that Derek Deane, who had joined The Royal Ballet resident company, and was in the same building. We'd meet in the canteen after class, which helped me to feel less like an interloper in this tight-knit family.

Michael and I had landed on our feet, having secured a basement flat in Upper Berkeley Street, W1 for a manageable rent of £5 per week. The flat was big by London standards and smack in the middle of the city, a short walk from Selfridge's and Oxford Street, the shopping centre of the world. Walking to Covent Garden or Carnaby Street was easy. We were chuffed. Our friends enjoyed the flat as much as we did, and it became a place where we all devoured copious amounts of Carlsberg Special Brew and Brandy Alexanders. There were many euphoric nights, enhanced by the odd marijuana brownie and Leonard Cohen crooning "Hallelujah".

* * *

The Royal Ballet had planned to move the Sadler's Wells Royal Ballet to a permanent rehearsal and performance space in Islington, a district north of Greater London. The year I joined the company, 1975, this plan was suddenly implemented, and Islington's Sadler's Wells Theatre was going to be our patch. In light of this, the time had come for us to move from our cosy, trendy basement flat, though we'd moved there just a few months before. Naturally, we felt sad to leave what had become our London party pad.

I cannot remember how we found the house at 176 New North Road, Islington, N1, but the moment we saw it we knew we had to have it. As Michael was freelancing with no regular income, I would need to shoulder the mortgage repayments, which meant that the prospect of acquiring the property came with some concern—but it was a leap of faith I had to take. I felt excited by that prospect. The house was a four-story Victorian terrace with a good-sized garden and sun deck. It was an absolute dream, and walking distance to Sadler's Wells Theatre. The previous American owners had done a top-to-toe renovation, with all the modern conveniences including a dishwasher, secondary glazing and skirting board central heating throughout. We instantly put the little house we'd purchased in Melbourne on the market and, thank goodness, it sold quickly, giving us the deposit we needed to seal the deal. We loved 176. It was the perfect place to host parties in our garden and on our sun deck that overlooked North London, and to while away summer vacations entertaining our assortment of colourful friends.

* * *

I did not possess the usual long-limbed, svelte physique typical of Royal Ballet dancers. Nonetheless, I needed to blend in—especially because my situation was uncommon, having entered the company on a coryphée contract with the promise of a promotion to soloist. This was difficult for other dancers, who felt overlooked as they'd been through the Royal Ballet training system and rightly felt they were in line for promotions that should not go to an outsider. In their eyes, the Royal Ballet management had broken rank. I understood their disappointment and learnt quickly how to deal with English frostiness. Fortunately, their coolness to me didn't last long, and they became my dearest, life-long friends.

This was a new world and I needed to watch my Ps and Qs, and for sure not get beyond my station. Stepping aside when a principal dancer walked by, never strutting across the studio in front of the ballet staff during a rehearsal and for goodness sake if the directors or, God forbid, the formidable Dame Ninette de Valois – former Director and founder of The Royal Ballet – should enter the room, do not speak.

Each day, I enjoyed observing the elegance of the ballet company. The principal dancers set the tone with graciousness and style, and the rest of us did our best to follow.

When learning a ballet from the company repertoire, the ballet staff were sticklers for getting every step exactly as the choreographer, dead or alive, had wanted. Woe betide anyone who even considered changing a step. I noticed the supreme level of respect for anything to do with the company; a standard upheld across the board.

The dancers, due to their Royal Ballet School education, had a sound knowledge of the history of the company. Their abiding love for its tradition and heritage was impressive. There were many cherished formalities: the stage manager, when running the show, dressed in evening suit and tie, and when the national anthem was played before curtain up the dancers behind the curtain would stop their pre-show practising and remain still and silent. No one ever disrespected their costume, which would be hung up after use exactly as it was found. The rules were stringent: you felt you might be burned at the stake for sitting in a costume, or eating in costume. Putting your hands on the hip basque of your tutu was taboo, as was tugging or handling the bodice of your tutu once it was on, which could result in extra washing of the tutu, thus adding wear and marking to the fabric. Protecting your tutus was absolutely essential, and getting on the wrong side of the wardrobe mistress was almost a fate worse than death. And, of course, nobody missed morning class unless they were dead. Speaking on stage during a performance, or on the side of the stage, was also forbidden, and there was to be no reading or talking to other dancers during a rehearsal or class. I had to learn the hierarchy of where to stand during the class, and never take a place at the barre usually occupied by a principal. Always required were spotless pink pointe shoes that made no noise on the stage. When travelling with the company smart clothing was expected, as well as a good stock of evening dresses for social events after performances, as we were to comport ourselves as ambassadors for Great Britain and The Royal Ballet.

Gosh, I had so much to remember, and so many ballets to learn: *The Rake's Progress, Checkmate, Les Patineurs, Façade, Pineapple Poll, Concerto, La Fille mal gardée, Elite Syncopations, The Invitation, La Boutique fantasque, Giselle* and *Les Sylphides*. Learning *Les Sylphides* was no problem. I knew every step. Madam, my wonderful teacher in Perth, had learnt it first-hand from the master who created it, Michel Fokine, and she handed it directly to her students. The same applied to *La Boutique fantasque*. When its choreographer, Léonide Massine, came to London to teach it to us he was charmed when I told him that Madam Kira Bousloff, or Kira Abricossova as she was known back then (the apricot they called her), had taught it to me impeccably. One thing I didn't mention to anyone is that I'd danced the leading role in *Giselle* in our school production when I was 14. I kept that quiet for fear of appearing beyond my station, which would never do!

The ballets we learned and danced belong to a large group of Royal Ballet heritage treasures, and I dared not get one step wrong. I was doing my best each day, but was still at a loss as to whether I was on the right track. Reassurance was not forthcoming; it was simply not Royal Ballet management style to offer encouragement. Dancers were expected to get on with it, which they did as a result of their Royal Ballet breeding.

However, advice was forthcoming on occasion. I remember one principal who had the longest, most beautiful ballet legs I'd ever seen; her name was Vyvyan Lorrayne. She was the loveliest person, always ready to help. There was one other extraordinary dancer by the name of Lynn Seymour, who arrived to rehearse *Las Hermanas,* a dramatic ballet choreographed by Kenneth MacMillan. She was MacMillan's muse, the dancer who most inspired him, and I was spellbound as she draped her limbs around every crevice of her partner's body, seemingly becoming part of him. There was no holding back, just complete abandonment. It was as if she could not hold back from immersing herself totally in the movement, in her character. I played a minor role to Lynn's leading role and looked on, spellbound, as she monopolised the studio with her intensity: stopping and starting, doing and redoing. She was vocal, teasing out every nuance and meaning of the choreographer's intention. Her constant questioning made sense to me, taking me back to my time working with Agnes de Mille. Lynn Seymour was a breed apart: intelligent, authentic, a total creature. I was riveted by her uniqueness. She danced and worked in ways I'd not seen before, and haven't seen since.

As I strove to better my own dancing, the revered ballerina Merle Park kindly offered advice, suggesting I work on my port de bras – the carriage of the arms – which was rather helter-skelter compared to the British correct placement. She seemed to like me, and I was grateful to her. Yet, although I was struggling internally and most of time winging my way, I was loving every moment.

* * *

However, even as my professional life was becoming more and more fulfilling, my life with Michael was beginning to fall apart. Gradually it was becoming painfully clear that his effeminacy, which I had found so attractive, ultimately portended a sexual preference that was destined to destroy our marriage. It was all so confusing: outwardly his effeminate body language defined him as unmistakeably gay, yet during intimacy he seemed heterosexual. Until that point, our sex life had been satisfactory, but I had begun to withdraw from it. This hurt and bothered him, as he desperately wanted things to remain as they'd always been. But that was becoming impossible for me. I hated this. I could feel Michael's pain. We loved each other dearly, but sex had never been the defining factor in our relationship and, in any case, as my physical attraction to him waned I knew there was nothing I could do about it.

There followed a time when I was able to ease my conscience. My withdrawing from sex freed Michael, allowing him to pursue the sexual satisfaction he needed. Watching him gravitate into his gay life was not difficult, and it affirmed what I long sensed: that he had perceived me more as a comforter than a lover. I could see that he was finding contentment, living the life he was supposed to live. Even so, this was a sad time. We were both in turmoil. We knew our lives needed to take divergent paths but our love for each other was deep. I knew I would miss him dreadfully. In my frayed state I'd even considered not divorcing him but continuing our life together on a new understanding. But, in truth, the romantically famished woman I had become was in need of sensual fulfilment and the sort of pleasure Michael could not provide.

PART THREE

DAVID

We all knew the principal dancer David Ashmole was transferring to Sadler's Wells Royal Ballet due to a lack of ballet performances at the Royal Opera House—a common situation at the time, as performances were shared with the opera, and ballet took second place to it. David was hungry, yearning for a more varied repertoire, and for as many performances as our director Peter Wright could throw at him. He was a pure, classical Royal Ballet dancer; the epitome of the elegant, beautiful ballet Prince. The corps de ballet women were aflutter when David arrived, and many of the higher-ranked dancers were smitten by this reserved creature who had no need to be the centre of attention off stage, whereas on stage there could be no doubt of his presence and command.

Sadler's Wells Royal Ballet had invested in a majestic new full-length production of *Swan Lake* choreographed by Peter Wright. This was a costly production, with magnificent costumes and décor. The prospect of its success hung heavily over us all. It had to work… and indeed it did. In my opinion, it is the finest production of *Swan Lake* created in the 20th century. I was cast as the Italian princess, and I still take pride in being part of the original cast. On opening night, with the leading roles danced by Galina Samsova as Odette/Odile and David Ashmole as Prince Siegfried, the atmosphere on stage and in the audience was nothing short of electric. Everyone in the theatre was captivated.

David's subdued off-stage manner was one I had recognised in others who excelled at what they did but felt no need to convince others of their talents. This was a quality I found intensely attractive in men and still do. Having been promoted to the position of principal dancer of The Royal Ballet in 1975, aged 26, he was one of the youngest dancers at that time to achieve the highest rank. There lay ahead a very long career for the top dancer that he was. The stage was David's space; he owned it.

The first time I saw David I knew I would love this man. His emotional remoteness made him so mysterious and attractive. I had to know what lay beneath it. Our glamorous world touring and the intimacy of rehearsals was an ideal place for our relationship to prosper. Our attraction to each other was enhanced by mutual respect, a shared work ethic and commitment. David was at the top of his game; the more performances he danced, the more he thrived. Hard work fed his adrenaline. No rehearsal was too long or too arduous to tackle. He'd been coached by one of the company's toughest, most unforgiving task masters, Michael Somes who, in a previous production, had danced Siegfried for years, opposite Margot Fonteyn. Somes rehearsed dancers almost to breaking point. His method did not suit everyone, and some dancers wilted under his demands. David also struggled, but remained forever grateful to Somes for fostering in him the backbone and the technique he needed to succeed.

As my relationship with David intensified, wrenching feelings of self-loathing were never far away. Though we sought to keep our relationship secret, we were fooling no one. The disapproval of most company members was no secret either. Weekend late-night parties on the road, laced with copious amounts of Carlsberg Special Brew, stoked our hankering for each other. The sneaky deception continued, along with mental anguish. I felt captured by the love of two men, a feeling that would not ease. Yet, at the same time, I was increasingly unavailable to Michael, who was living in fear of abandonment. I felt deeply for him, yet knew I could no longer live with him. I moved downstairs into our small rental basement flat in the hope that I could wean him off loving me so that he would let me go free. Instead, his mental state continued to deteriorate, his despair tearing away at the three of us when he declared he would kill himself if I left him. Daytime stalking and night-time appearances out of nowhere were frequent. My fears worsened and my guilt increased. Should I stay with Michael for fear that he might carry out his threats of suicide? What did I owe him? What did I owe David? What did I owe myself? Did I have any right to be happy at the cost of Michael's misery?

As the months passed, Michael plummeted further into depression, and did attempt suicide on two occasions. My terror of being the cause of his death left me feeling desperate. I knew that Michael was capable of ending his life. Losing me was hard enough, but losing me to the talented, beautiful, successful David Ashmole was crushing every part of his being. But I could not deceive myself about what my heart wanted: to be beside David, safely wrapped in his quiet tenderness. One night I ran away from the house and booked into a hotel in Islington. I called David, who I knew by then to be a natural, loving caretaker. He arrived as soon as he could. That night it was clear to me that my married life with Michael had ended. The following weeks were spent sleeping on friends' sofas and making sure I had all I needed in my car. Michael was in a shattered state; there were more suicide threats, which on one occasion landed him in hospital. I cannot be sure, even now, if his attempts to take his own life were cries for help or an effort to manipulate me into staying with him. What I clearly remember is that when I called the hospital and asked if his condition was serious, I was icily told, "We take all suicide attempts seriously."

The prospect of leaving Michael was a heartbreaking decision; our love for each other had felt unbreakable. Would I ever be rid of the attachment and love I felt for him? Though his gayness had driven me away, I was constantly reminded that it was his kind, feminine side that had been so appealing when we met and married; it was a large part of what I loved so much about him. His quick wit, sense of humour, outrageous thinking, love and knowledge of art and all things beautiful... how could I live without him?

Each day, each hour, I ping-ponged between grieving for my life with Michael and longing for David. I could not imagine how was I going to navigate anything in this state, but then soon David and I were back on tour, feeling desperate for each other. Still swamped in feelings of helplessness and shame, I tumbled back into David's awaiting arms. The truth was that he, like me, was involved in another relationship, yet the raw magnetism between us was undeniable, and drawing us together.

We continued to rehearse and perform, which provided momentary relief from our anguish. At other times, the weight of what had eventuated pushed me further and further into a black hole. Although the word depression was seldom spoken in those days, I was clearly depressed, and one evening I asked David if he would kill me. I felt broken. Somehow, I knew I needed to take drastic action. And that was when I finally started divorce proceedings.

Previously, when I had suggested divorce, Michael had resisted. But now he was able to accept it. We grieved deeply. Michael was the most interesting person I'd ever known, and I had found there is something undeniably special about the love a homosexual man can give to a woman. And so, with heaviness of heart, our marriage ended. We shed many tears in each other's arms, along with sudden doses of harsh, angry words, but always we'd forgive and resolve those moments with embraces and caressing. During this time I needed the warmth of friendship, and depended on a few close friends for comfort, but it could not ease my shame. I knew my integrity was in question, and that hurt. It appeared to everyone that I had walked out on funny, smart, entertaining Michael. Looking back with hard-earned wisdom I ask myself if I had known when I met Michael what I came to know would I have acted differently? The answer is yes: I would have recognised the sort of all-male relationship Michael needed, and I would never have married him.

Somehow, David and I managed to get through the storm. But then, one night, driving back to London, our car skidded on black ice and toppled over, landing upside down in a field. I remember shuddering as I watched David wedge his way out from underneath the upturned car. Was this accident a punishment for what I had done to Michael? Perhaps it was. And perhaps we deserved it. But we continued thrashing on.

* * *

Sadler's Wells Royal Ballet was a touring company, which meant we were constantly in transit. Our domestic life was crammed into short London performances and rehearsal weeks, leaving little time for socialising. Bags and suitcases forever littered the hallway, at the ready for a coming world or provincial tour. Always at the back of our minds lingered our lovely summer break in Greece, when our time was dedicated solely to each other and only backpacks were required.

The more we were together, the deeper our bond became, and the more David revealed himself, despite his usual reluctance to explore or disclose his deepest feelings. I believe

59

this discomfort resulted from the trauma of his mother abandoning him when was four years old. From then on, it seems, shutting down became a safe place he came to know well. My deep love for David granted me the patience I needed to tease out gently his fear of repeated abandonment. In time, he would come to feel emotionally safe enough to share his childhood wounds with me, and even to cherish the small, lonely boy he once was.

Professionally we had been compatible from the start of our relationship, as we both understood and accepted the demands of working and living together, and were mindful of each other's responsibilities. The bedrock of our personal relationship was caring for each other's needs, mentally and physically. Our mutual term of endearment was "Nutty", taken from a character in the May Gibbs book series *Snugglepot and Cuddlepie*—the book my mother used to read to me, and on which, a few years later, I would base the first ballet I choreographed.

Looking back at my years with David I cannot recall a time when we were not attracted to each other and in love. I'm very sure of this, because my torturous ache for him lasted for such a long time after he died.

* * *

In 1982 we bought a beautiful Victorian four-story house in Finsbury Park, making it our London forever home, or at least that was the idea. The house was full to exploding with Victoriana furnishings, countless pieces of the Moorcroft pottery David so avidly collected and precious items—among them antique books on ballet, theatre design, costume design and old ballet programmes we'd bought in many cities while touring the world. It seemed to us that everything was going our way. Despite our peripatetic life, buying the house seemed to thrust us into nesting mode, to the degree that nesting was possible.

* * *

We had been living together for eight years when Sadler's Wells Royal Ballet embarked on a lengthy Asian and Australian tour. By this time, David, who always craved a challenge, was eager to expand beyond the familiar repertoire of The Royal Ballet. He had danced so many performances of ballets he loved like *Giselle* and *Swan Lake* and performed a vast assortment of other lovely works, among them *Coppélia, The Two Pigeons, La Fille mal gardée, Prodigal Son, La Bayadère, The Sleeping Beauty, Daphnis and Chloë, Symphonic Variations, Song of the Earth, Elite Syncopations, Concerto, Dances at a Gathering*. In *Checkmate*, a ballet choreographed by Dame Ninette de Valois, he danced the famous Red Knight—a role he became well known for due to his pristine technique and musicality. David had brilliant instincts about ballet in general, and his own dancing in particular and, at one rehearsal of *Checkmate*, Dame Ninette stopped him in the middle of his Red Knight solo and scolded him, claiming he had changed the choreography of one sequence. David would never dream of changing a choreographer's work and, in any case, dancers were strictly forbidden from altering choreography. Having danced the role numerous times, he was certain he was performing the proper steps, but one did not argue with Madam. So when she gave him a different sequence of steps, insisting they were the right ones, he politely took her corrections on board and did what she demanded. But, back in the dressing room, he was rolling his eyes and telling me she was wrong. The following day, during the stage rehearsal, he dutifully danced the steps Madam had insisted upon. When the rehearsal ended, Madam came hurrying onto the stage calling, "Ashmole, Ashmole. I was completely wrong. Go back to what you were doing."

* * *

Because David was so desirous to explore the works of new choreographers and different productions, he was thinking of leaving Sadler's Wells Royal Ballet. The company that most appealed to him was The Australian Ballet so, while performing in Melbourne, he invited Marilyn Rowe to attend one of his performances, with the thought of using it as an audition. Marilyn was a revered former ballerina with The Australian Ballet who'd lately been appointed the company's acting director by the Australian Ballet Board. At Marilyn's request, Gailene Stock, Director of the National Theatre Ballet School in Victoria, had been given leave, and was assisting Marilyn in steering the company. They both thought David would be a fine fit for The Australian Ballet but, as Interim Director, Marilyn was not able to offer him a contract. So we had to wait and see who the incoming director would be.

At the end of tour, as we flew out of Perth en route back to the UK, David told me that he wanted us to move to Australia, that it was where we should be living. He was smitten with the country, its people, its landscape and its more relaxed, sun-filled way of life. But returning to Australia had never been my intention. I'd made my home in London with no thoughts of relocating. I was turning 39, intending to retire at the end of the season. We were both keen to complete our life by allowing ourselves the opportunity starting a family. Relocating could wait, or so I thought.

One week later we got a call from Maina Gielgud, a former dancer and the niece of John Gielgud, who'd just been appointed Artistic Director of The Australian Ballet.

She asked David to come to the Savoy hotel and meet with her. I knew at that moment we were on the move. David arrived back at the house beaming from ear to ear and, with one big hug, lifting and swirling me around the kitchen announcing, "Nutty darling we're off to Melbourne!" Phew! Deal done... I was locked into this change of life, and decided there and then to go to Australia willingly.

At this time in our lives, we were in very different places professionally. In my mind I had already retired. I was busily thinking ahead about teaching, choreographing and motherhood. During the previous 12 months I'd occasionally been taken by surprise when certain technical steps I'd been able to do instinctively suddenly let me down. I'd been a natural turner, known for my ability to execute multiple pirouettes; what on earth was happening? The more I tried to locate my natural ease at turning, the more it eluded me. Being tiny in stature allowed me the swiftness I needed to get my legs around fast-moving roles, but I had become alarmed as my speed lessened and my technique felt increasingly murky. Clearly my performance days were coming to an end, but that was fine with me. I'd had a massively long career, all of it injury free, and had danced literally hundreds of performances and dozens of ballets. I had danced as much as I needed to. The burden of ambition had gone. I was free and ready to explore other ideas and plans.

David was different. He had launched hundreds of opening nights as we toured worldwide. Over the years we had performed in Canada, the USA and throughout Europe, as well as in Malaysia, South Korea, Australia, New Zealand, Japan, China and Russia. Our touring was endless, as we returned to many countries over and over again. Now, at 36, he was at his dancing peak, technically and artistically. He was also aware that maintaining his present high standard was going to be a challenge. His hunger for work and exploring new ballets never wavered, nor did his passion for performing. He was not fazed by the looming reality that soon his technique would, inevitably, enter a downward slope. He simply focussed on working to his best and embracing every performance that came his way. When enmeshed in his work, David's quiet happiness was palpable, especially after a performance he'd really enjoyed, of which there were many. He particularly loved the roles of Albrecht in *Giselle*, Prince Siegfried in *Swan Lake*, Prodigal Son, Romeo and many more. His fulfilment meant so much to me, as it gently filtered into our life together, enhancing it with contentment and peacefulness.

David met with Peter Wright, Director of Sadler's Wells Royal Ballet, to let him know our decision. The management were not happy to be losing David, one of their major principal dancers, but everyone made light of it, which was okay. When the ballet season ended in July 1984, it was time to leave. We put our beautiful Victorian home on the market, and it sold almost instantly. David, ever the dedicated collector, wanted to take everything we owned with us; nothing was to be left behind. Miraculously, The Australian Ballet provided professional packers to come to the house to wrap and pack every single piece of antique furniture, paintings and house wares. What a godsend; we were grateful for their consideration and generosity.

*** *** ***

At last we were on our Qantas flight to Melbourne, enjoying glasses of champagne as we recalled the life we'd been gifted: travelling the world, dancing in the grandest of opera houses and theatres. We had shared memories of glamorous receptions attended by the glitterati and, often, the royalty of whichever country we were in at the time. We laughed as we remembered the night The Royal Navy's top brass had come to our performance and how, the next day, we all accepted their irresistible invitation to join the officers on board the submarine Dreadnought, anchored offshore in the port of Thessaloniki, near to where we were performing. The Royal Navy and Sadler's Wells Royal Ballet: what a marriage! The press loved it! And, as we sipped still more champagne, we agreed that our life dedicated to a ballet company had presented us with global travel and a lifetime of experiences that surely outweighed the strain of the body-breaking work demanded of us as ballet dancers.

David was thrilled as he imagined our new life. As we would soon see, the standard of the company's dancers was exceptional, and boasted a clutch of hungry, hot-shot young males. All reaching for the stars, their technique was influenced by the dazzling and enigmatic Mikhail Baryshnikov, who had defected to the West from the Soviet Union's Kirov Ballet. David knew those ankle-snappers would be fast on his heels. He relished the prospect, saying their energy and hunger was the force he needed to propel him through the next few years of his dancing life. As it turned out, his role-model presence inspired the youngsters, who were eager to learn from him, and they in turn ignited his formidable will to stay on top for as long as he could.

Quietly fearless, David's way was to rehearse and rehearse, working meticulously until his dancing was as stellar as it needed to be—something Michael Somes had drilled into him. It was only at that point that I could see he'd entered performance mode, ready to embrace the stage with all his might. Nothing and no one could be in his way.

* * *

Top-ranking, pure classical dancers are a rare breed. They live with the knowledge that there are no short cuts; their classical technique must be as finely moulded and sharp as cut crystal, and they must also have the physical and mental ability to entice and hold public attention. Their high-ranking position requires nerves of steel, the curiosity of a cat and an available, tender heart. Many possess a natural dance instinct and invest in the filigree of the steps beyond their basic technique. Some are blessed with an inborn knowing of accent and musical phrasing, which comes from their own natural, musical impulse. They are elite athletes, dedicated to strengthening every part of their body—that precious instrument they rely on to interpret music through movement night after night.

As performance dates drew nearer, I would feel David's need to withdraw. I knew the signals. I'd experienced that same need for head space myself. Don't touch me; dust all around me and leave me in peace. Before curtain up, David would be the first dancer on the stage, sometimes quietly walking through his entrances, more often not moving but poised in contemplation, thinking through his responses, still working out a sequence he felt he needed to polish, or simply getting a feel for the stage. Other members of the company, including stage staff and directors, would pick up on his body language and leave him alone and in peace. David maintained his thorough training and understanding of how his body worked in relation to music. His excellent coordination and ideal body proportions had prevented him from serious injury. He was protective of his finely tuned limbs knowing that, should his workload go into overdrive – which frequently happens in a large ballet company – it would be time to pull back and listen to his body.

From the moment David arrived at The Australian Ballet, what excited him most was that the works they presented were eclectic and so diverse: their solid collection of the classics was embellished by a broad range of works by international choreographers, and he would go on to shine in ballets he'd never performed before, among them John Cranko's *Onegin*, Maurice Béjart's *Songs of a Wayfarer*, Jerome Robbins's *In the Night* and comic ballet *The Concert*, Jiří Kylián's *Forgotten Land*, Glen Tetley's *Voluntaries* and Tetley's *Orpheus*, which would be created on him. So now, joy of joys, he had a whole new repertoire to work with, and master.

* * *

Soon after we arrived in Australia, Maina asked me to join her ballet staff as Assistant to the Artistic Director. It seemed like a good idea. Australia was working well for us both, David relishing his new repertoire while I was loving the opportunity to work on every level of such a large company. Part of my job was teaching and coaching the dancers, which was incredibly rewarding. I couldn't get enough of time in the studio. As I had the company's brightest etoiles at hand, I took the opportunity to choreograph a showcase pas de deux for David McAllister and Elizabeth Toohey. I named it *La Favorita*, and it would become a popular fixture at galas. In addition, I watched almost every performance and assisted Maina with casting and whatever issues arrived on a daily basis, which absorbed many hours of my time. I'd made the transition from dancer to management with ease, and never once yearned to be back on the stage.

David had found us a lovely house in the leafy suburb of Keilor, and he'd gone ahead and arranged our wedding. The company were to perform in my hometown of Perth later that year, so our wedding took place there, on a beautiful Sunday afternoon. My parents were fond of David, whose English manners and calm approach to life charmed them. His obvious devotion to me offered them assurance that I would be loved and cared for. At some point before the wedding David had spoken privately to my father, who was deeply touched by this somewhat old-fashioned gesture. I imagine David wanted to show respect to my father and seek his blessing. My mother observed that whenever I was with David my playfulness bubbled over. I'm not sure I was conscious of this, though playful I was on our wedding day. I wore a very delicate, rather sheer '20s crystal beaded dress with a beanie headdress dripping with crystals and pearls. My father's eyes twinkled with tears when he saw me, and I remember laughing all day as friends, family and some of the dancers joined us for what was a most glorious occasion.

* * *

One day, one of the dancers casually mentioned some weird disease that was killing gay people in the United States. Although this sounded dramatic, no one seemed to pay much attention to it. We just got on with our lives.

Around this time, Michael wrote to me, saying that he was taking three months off to spend time in San Francisco. On his return to London he called me and said he'd been unwell and had made an appointment to see his doctor. He called again a few days later to tell me he was HIV positive. I remember the shattering feeling that overtook my body, and the raspy breath that came out of my mouth. David's sturdy arms were suddenly holding me as I tried to contain my horror at Michael's news. Having read up on the AIDS virus by then, I was aware that this monster would soon be ripping into him. He was already becoming weaker, needing blood top-ups constantly. He'd started on the only available drug, AZT, and was struggling with its side effects. I was terribly concerned for him.

Sometime before Michael's visit to San Francisco I had become aware that he'd gravitated into the underbelly of London's gay life, becoming overtly glib about his sexuality while being drawn into the precarious world of gay men in hiding. Leading an undercover existence came with fear and anxiety; reprimand and homophobic putdowns were a constant threat. The cruel exclusion gay men felt was palpable—and so they huddled together in bars, pubs and clubs seeking the safety of like-minded males, a culture Michael fitted into with ease. He attracted extraordinary, outrageous people, blessed with humour and a forked tongue capable of reducing others to feeling humdrum and mundane. He had enjoyed relaying his weekend escapades to me, littering our conversations with jokes about copious amounts of alcohol and drug fuelled all-nighters. I had often been stunned by what I was hearing. And though I concluded that Michael's lifestyle was deliberate, and he loved it, to me it had seemed menacing.

So, once again, my mind, heart and thoughts were consumed by two fates: Michael's, as he approached what was certain to be his death, and the fate I shared with David, as we sought, time and again, to bring new life into the world.

* * *

Two years had passed since we'd first begun trying to get pregnant. I was 41 by this time, David was 38, and both of us were at our wits end. We yearned for our very own tiny baby, and the effort of constant trying every which way was taking a massive toll on us. We experimented with diet changes, mucus tests, ovulation cycles, but it seemed that nothing on God's earth was going to get us where we desperately needed to be. Yet, despite our trauma in trying to conceive a baby, David was flourishing professionally—maintaining his position in the company and navigating his way through The Australian Ballet's repertoire. I was still enjoying working alongside Maina and developing working relationships throughout the company. As Assistant to the Artistic Director my job was more or less open ended, and though I loved the work, my anxiety about getting pregnant had left me looking skeletal and secretly knowing that the only thing that deeply, urgently mattered to me was having David's baby inside me.

We had created a warm, safe place to live in Melbourne, and our lovely four-bedroom house, blessed with sunshine, was the perfect setting in which to bring up our child. I had navigated the local nursery and its amenities, which were more than ideal. The place was perfect: a proper baby land crammed with chatty mums and church hall Christmas events, including the arrival of Father Christmas in a big red fire truck courtesy of the local fire brigade.

In 1986, two years after we'd arrived in Melbourne, my bedside evening reading was *Your Baby and Child* by Dr Penelope Leach. Her book had become the new-age manual for dealing with babies and toddlers. Every young mother had a copy. I was leaving no stone unturned preparing for our longed-for little one to arrive. Doctors suggested we take a break. We needed peace of mind and some relaxation, they said, to give ourselves a fair chance. But, due to our respective ages, I was fearful that time was stacked against us. Tangled thoughts set me doubting David's love for me. Perhaps, I fretted, he no longer found me attractive and that explained why he was unable to get me pregnant.

While this struggle continued, I was corresponding with Michael many times a week. His HIV had morphed into AIDS, and his awareness of what inevitably awaited him plunged him into depression. He was relying on the Buddhist practice of daily chanting and a self-help book by Louise Hay, *You Can Heal Your Life,* which seemed to calm his anxiety and ease his anguish. It was Hay who coined the affirmation "It's only a thought and a thought can be changed", a reminder I have tucked away in my own survival kit. As for Michael, it was his hope that he would reach a point when he could calmly entrust his destiny to the universe.

* * *

Christmas was upon us. The Australian Ballet closed for their annual vacation. My niece Carina and her family were coming from Perth to spend Christmas with David and me, bringing their son Michael and newborn baby girl Lydia with them. That December was especially hot in Melbourne. Our lovely home overlooking Brimbank Nature Reserve was flooded with sunlight, and our pool sparkled. Carina, her husband Frank, Michael and baby Lydia arrived—the adults laden with champagne, lobsters and baby gear. During warm, sultry nights spent around our pool, Carina and I engaged in long conversations while David and Frank played pool in our games room. Early mornings were joyful. Carina would bring tiny Lydia into our bed and there, David and I and the baby would cat nap. These were lovely times that lulled us into imagining how it might be to have a baby of our own to love and cuddle.

At the start of the new year, we were back at work and well into the new season when, one morning, I awoke feeling unwell with painful nipples. In those days, there were no home pregnancy tests, so I charged out the door, dashing to our local GP, who'd previously done three pregnancy tests on me, all of them negative. As I trembled at the thought that this was another false alarm, our doctor looked at me and confirmed that I was pregnant. I begged him to tell me he was absolutely sure. Could the test have been wrong? He was a kindly man who gave me the warmest smile I will remember forever. I drove back to the studio where David was taking morning class. He looked over at me as I walked in and knew immediately that we were expecting.

We were in full bloom, in a state of euphoria, adoring the knowledge that inside of me was a tiny life to be loved and looked after by us. I stopped smoking, gave up alcohol; food tasted better, and I was enjoying my work apart from the odd morning feeling slightly sick. I was flooding with hormones, and we both were feeling we'd achieved something miraculous. David, forever the caretaker, yearned to be a father and now his wish was granted.

As soon as I became pregnant my best friend, Margaret Mercer, decided she wanted to be pregnant too, which she achieved almost immediately. Another friend, Marilyn Rowe, also found herself pregnant. There we were, about to be late mothers of the same age. I'd been collecting baby clothes from around the world while on tour, and the collection was enormous. I loved sorting through the tiny pieces, which triggered memories of where I'd bought them. Life was full of hope.

At four months into my pregnancy, I'd not been feeling well, so I asked to see my doctor who ordered an ultrasound. I went by myself, as I'd had this procedure before, and was not overly concerned until the technician left the room and returned with another nurse. Gently, she told me she could find no heartbeat. I don't remember getting to our home but, somehow, I drove myself to Keilor. Nor do I recall how I told David; I just know he suddenly arrived home. We were in utter despair, shattered, inconsolable, questioning how this could be happening to us. Our little baby had died and was still inside me, warm and loved. I did not know how to be or think; I searched for my survival instinct, which I could not find. The hospital called and booked me into the Royal Woman's Hospital for a procedure the next morning. That night and the following days were filled with bitter tears and quiet sobbing, a harrowing sound I would experience many times in my life, unbeknownst to me at the time. Sadness, loss and disappointment plummeted me into despair.

* * *

Work continued and the company moved to Sydney for a long season at the Opera House. I made out that I was fine, presenting my get-up, dress-up, show-up face. David was quiet; an unspoken sadness seemed to surround him.

We had been in Sydney just a few days, when I told David I thought I was still pregnant; my nipples were sore, and my breasts were swollen. David was kind and supportive telling me this 'pregnancy' was in my mind. But I could not stop thinking that perhaps they had all made a terrible error. Could I have been pregnant with twins? Or was I losing my mind? I called my doctor in Melbourne, who seemed not to disbelieve me and told me to see a gynaecologist he recommended in Sydney. I made the appointment for the next day. It turned out that I had not been suffering from a phantom pregnancy. My urine test showed positive and I was producing the pregnancy hormone HCG (Human Chorionic Gonadotropin). I was immediately diagnosed with having had a hydatidiform mole pregnancy—a rare condition more likely to occur in women over 35. My Melbourne doctor wanted me back in his care as soon as possible. I flew there early the next morning in a state of turmoil.

I needed help. I was falling apart. David flew back to Melbourne. We were told future pregnancies were out of the question as the condition, at my age, would more than likely happen again. My HCG levels were high and needed to come down otherwise chemotherapy would be essential to prevent potential tumours from invading other parts of my body. I was to stay in Melbourne, having blood tests every few days. My HCG levels were stubborn and not budging.

David and I were called to a meeting with my doctor and an oncologist, during which the oncologist stated that chemotherapy seemed necessary as we needed to arrest any tumours lurking in my body. At the very end of this meeting, my doctor suggested we wait a little longer before going for chemotherapy. I loved him at that moment. Maybe he felt my pain as he'd known what losing our baby and the recent weeks of confusion and uncertainty had done to me. Fearing the prospect of chemotherapy I asked whether, if my HCG levels did not fall but I chose not to have chemotherapy, there were any other options? The answer was that there were none.

It took a few weeks, but finally my HCG levels began to slide slowly downwards. Still, each day, I poked and prodded my body searching for tumours that could be lurking within me. Our plans for having our own tiny baby had crumbled. We knew we were out of options, and it hurt. For the first time I witnessed disturbing fear in David's eyes as he absorbed the precarious state of my health. We clung to each other, lost in uncertainty. My strong, dependable David was wavering. I felt him shudder at night as we held onto each other, longing for sleep—the only escape that brought relief from our pain. I knew that once David went back into the studio he'd find comfort in doing what he did best. The brutal physicality and mental endurance needed to execute what was demanded of him would act as a distraction and keep him upright.

On his first morning back at work I cried as I watched him walk to the car. His downtrodden body language was shocking, and new to me. But I was comforted by the knowledge that David instinctively protected himself by detaching from emotional hurt. I'd seen him do it when we'd spoken of how his own motherless childhood had affected him. As for myself, I knew I just had to find a way to get on with it. But that way was elusive.

While I struggled in this darkness with this loss, the pregnancies of my two friends were textbook good. I was doing my trooper act at which I was practised, but inside I was destroying myself with envy and rage. How was I going to continue to be kind and supportive to my friends when I didn't want to see either of them? My thoughts were irrational and all consuming. The sight of a swollen pregnant woman erupted mean thoughts in my head, and I wanted to shout out, "Even you, looking like you do, someone managed to make you pregnant; how did that happen?" I was spiralling out of control.

My two friends knew I was suffering and were gentle with me. I did not want to lose their friendship: I'd known Margaret since we were 12 years old. She was my closest friend, and she asked if I would be willing to be with her at the birth. Her request was understandable, but unanswerable; it seemed too big an ask. If I agreed to it, how much would witnessing that event increase my pain and longing? But if I refused to be there would it not create a gap between us, risking a friendship I truly cherished? Finally, I knew I had to be there to welcome this little baby. She was going to be part of my life and, after weeks of inner turmoil, my decision to attend felt okay.

One afternoon, while taking a rehearsal on stage, a message arrived telling me Margaret was in labour. Without hesitation I ran from the theatre into a taxi and arrived at the foot of her bed. There was no doubt in my mind that this was exactly where I needed to be. Margaret howled like an animal in distress. I'd never heard a sound like that before, and it shook me. She was locked in a place of endless pain, where no one could reach her. Jessie's wet head appeared slowly and steadily; she was not going to stop sliding gently out of Margaret. I was stuck in an emotion that was new to me. Maybe this was the "women's business" spoken of by

Aboriginal women, who relate it to a tribal connection and strength that exists between women, who learn from each other—handing on life's traditions and skills. At last, Margaret delivered a brand-new baby into our tribe. When the nurse placed this tiny, damp bundle in my arms and I looked down at Jessie's perfect face I felt a flood of love for her. The memory of Jessie's birth has comforted me many times. It confirmed that I still had my inner strength, which had allowed me to let go of my resentment and mean-spiritedness and warm to this baby girl.

* * *

Life had moved on; my blood tests would continue for another year, after which I'd be given a clean bill of health. Processing the knowledge that David and I were never going to have a baby of our own, we decided to adopt. We were told that the process was lengthy and challenging, but we were energised and excited at the thought. From our perspective, we were ideal candidates. I'd retired, we had a lovely four-bedroom home with a garden in a gentle suburb of Melbourne. David was in full-time work, and we had a healthy stash of money. We were convinced our knowledge of life and travel would be in our favour. We were wrong. As it turned out, we were not even in line for consideration. Our ages were against us. The rejection offended me. I took exception at not being considered good enough, young enough or whatever it was. My understanding had been that, in order to adopt, you had to be able to provide a lovely home to a needy baby. I had no doubt that David and I could do this, and do it with tremendous love. But that didn't matter. According to the adoption service, we were too old.

* * *

Work rolled on for us with The Australian Ballet. As assistant to Maina Gielgud, the Artistic Director, I loved working closely with dancers and everyone on all levels of this large ballet company. Maina and I were well suited, both as a team and artistically. However, her management style was often perceived by dancers as biased and intrusive, which caused dissatisfaction amongst the company and resulted in my becoming the go-between, which is often the case with dancers, ballet staff and the director.

Navigating my way between Maina and the dancers was fraught with difficulties. Dancers sought fairness when it came to casting, and Maina made no bones about choosing dancers she preferred. Either she genuinely believed her casting was best for the public, or she was unable to bypass her attraction to certain dancers. I still don't know which it was. However, without doubt this was a time of unrest within the company and left many dancers feeling unfairly passed over. I would find myself stuck in the middle of serious and sensitive issues. I tried to pacify the dancers, explaining that the director's job was to choose the best dancer for each role, while also explaining to Maina that her casting choices were seen as favouritism. Maina would not back down and became even more determined to cast the ballets her way, which inflamed the situation even more. She seemed to enjoy the ensuing havoc. Her ability to ride out every storm was annoying, but somehow impressive for its unapologetic doggedness.

I decided to put forward an idea to The Australian Ballet for a work I wanted to choreograph. It would be a ballet based on *Snugglepot and Cuddlepie*, the Australian children's book series loved and adored not only by me throughout my childhood, but by thousands of others across many generations. The series was written by the much-treasured author May Gibbs, who was Australia's answer to Beatrix

Potter. She was an Englishwoman who had fallen in love with Australia's ecology and become fascinated by the interaction of plants and living things and the influence they have on human beings. One of her messages is particularly dear to me: "Humans please be kind to all bush creatures and do not pull flowers up by their roots." When writing the tales of *Snugglepot and Cuddlepie*, she had created illustrations based on Australian wildlife. Her beguiling images leapt off the pages into the minds of children— sparking their imaginations as mine had been sparked by them years before.

Maina and her board of directors jumped at my idea for this ballet, and immediately sought permission from the May Gibbs estate for the work to be created. With permission obtained, a budget was sorted and finance for the production secured by way of the Bicentennial Celebration Fund. It was decided that the ballet should be a full-length work set to an original score, which gave me the lengthy task of listening to endless recordings of Australian composers. I finally decided on Richard Mills, who agreed to be Composer-in-Residence while writing the music. How lucky was I to have the opportunity of having my own composer at my fingertips! My choice for creating the sets and costumes was Hugh Colman, one of Australia's leading theatre, opera and dance designers. I threw myself into selecting the scenes and blocking in my mind the ballet sequences. Weekends and after-work hours were spent with Richard around the piano as I sketched out solos and ensemble dances. Richard would play and we'd stop and start with me dancing, giving him tempi and lengths of each section.

Hearing only the piano, I had a hard time trying to imagine the completed score. Once the orchestra was in full flight, would the sound be as I'd dreamed? I fretted constantly, asking Richard where the harp cascade was; though I trusted and admired him, I could not imagine what he was doing with the score. To me, his music, played on the rehearsal piano, sounded like mere noise. All I could do was give the dancers counts to hang onto. Despite Richard reassuring me that every sound I'd asked for would be heard in his score, I dreaded the first full orchestral rehearsal, as I had no idea if I or my dancers would recognise the music they'd been dancing to for months. I stood near to Richard as he picked up his baton and the orchestra played the overture. Immediately I knew all was well; that the music was everything I'd hoped for and more. Tears of relief and gratitude coursed down my face as dear Richard looked over to me with a loving and comforting smile that said, *I promised you, and here it is*. I will never forget that moment. Not ever.

One of the special things about choreographing this ballet was that David was cast in it. He would portray a large fish named John Dory. It was a role he enjoyed as it was free from technical demands due to a wonderful, albeit cumbersome, headpiece and an elaborate, scaly costume, which somewhat restricted the choreography. The essence of the role was to depict the important presence of this large fish in contrast to the exquisite little fish named Obelia, whom John Dory loved. Hugh Colman's exquisite costumes prompted great excitement amongst the dancers, in particular the ravishing flower costumes and the costume for the snake, which looked suitably slimy and scary. The dancers' excitement was palpable as they tried out the fit and feel of their costumes while in motion.

We had two stage rehearsals before opening. During the last stage call, as I was polishing the final sequences, one of the dancers came to the foot of the stage and spewed vile abuse at me, telling me in front of the company, and in the most appalling way, exactly what he thought of my ballet. I was exhausted, frozen, unable to respond. Previously I had seen not even the slightest hint of this dancer's distress. Throughout the rehearsal period my entire cast had been patient and attentive; we'd shared many laughs as we navigated the music together, so this unexpected tirade came as a shock. David had witnessed it, but experience told him to remain silent and not inflame the situation. He was aware of my anxious state, but he also knew the dancer had crossed a professional line and, as he would kindly assure me later, the only person damaged by the outburst was the dancer himself. In the end, this incident taught me an important lesson about the value of not crumbling, and of persevering no matter the obstacle. Though I'd been stunned, felt deflated and was left questioning how the hell I was going to keep going, I knew I needed to remain steady and supportive of my dancers who'd worked so hard to bring my ballet to life.

Snugglepot and Cuddlepie premiered successfully at the Sydney Opera House on a hot summer evening—weather that seemed entirely appropriate for this danced rendition of the bush tales. The air seemed thick with nostalgia as the captivated audience tripped down memory lane, recalling bedtime stories well-known and loved by Australians. On that opening night, the ballet was all I could have wished for: the music was perfect, the dancers were wonderful and Hugh Colman's magical designs were praised and applauded. He had imbued the sets and costumes with every image and idea I'd shared with him. Australians are proud of their flora and fauna, protective of their vast, overwhelming landscape and – when the worst happens, and their land is ravaged by unstoppable bushfires – the whole nation weeps. And, for the audience on that summer night, *Snugglepot and Cuddlepie* was a vivid and lovely reminder of their deeply rooted earthy culture.

And so, what had been the worst year since losing our baby turned out to be a time of nourishment for me. I had been privileged to create a ballet especially for children. This was what I needed: speaking to children through my work replaced, in some ways, the absence of my own child. My rewards were many. Schools used the ballet as an educational tool, introducing children to the literature of May Gibbs and also to theatre, music and dance. The ballet's success meant that it remained in The Australian Ballet Dancer's Company repertoire for many years. I will always be grateful that the ballet of *Snugglepot and Cuddlepie* was, for so many children, the rich experience that the books of May Gibbs were for me.

* * *

After the Sydney season in 1987, the company came back to Melbourne, and rehearsals continued as usual. I was spending long hours in the studio doing what I did best, when Maina and the managing director, Noel Pelly asked to speak to me. Without explanation they told me that my contribution would no longer be required. I will never forget the feeling of disbelief I experienced. I felt broken into tiny pieces yet again. I left the building with tears streaming down my face. I was banished, crushed and bewildered.

David was outraged. To him, my dismissal was utterly uncalled for and deeply offensive. As he saw it, the Australian Ballet management had disgraced themselves, disrespected his wife and consequently caused a fissure that would never be repaired. But, even as his icy, English disapproval emerged in full force, his impeccable work ethic and professional commitment to the company never diminished. And that was as it ought to be, for his work was the sustenance he needed to survive, now more than ever, during yet another time of endurance for us. I was grateful that his dancing could provide him with the joy and solace he needed.

I was also grateful that David knew how to lessen my hurt, as he reminded me of qualities he loved so much about me: my quirkiness, my sharp humour, my need for getting things done, my insatiable appetite for ballet and, most of all, the never-failing passion I had for him—something I had no control over, and never ever held back. Yet, despite David's efforts, I spent much of the following year curled up in the house trying to find myself. Where was I? No baby, no job and feeling punished for what? I searched for answers but found none. Sadness, feelings of exclusion and abandonment weakened every part of my body. The only place I could find safety was in my bed, day after day. No explanation was ever offered by The Australian Ballet, and for a time I considered suing for unfair dismissal, but I was depleted and knew that were I to take on the establishment I'd be doomed to fail. David stood staunchly by me. He was stunned by the injustice of it and certain that nothing I had done could have warranted such a grandiose, painful gesture. He fumed that I had been betrayed and dismissed without negotiation, explanation or warning.

I understood what I needed to do; I had to find a way to recapture the brave me, the woman who at 18 fearlessly hopped on a ship and sailed alone to England bursting with hope. I longed to reconnect with that bold person who, with no safety net and against all odds, ended up getting a contract with The Royal Ballet. But could I do this?

The following months passed slowly. Finally, the fog engulfing me began to lift when I started teaching at a small, local ballet school, which provided a measure of mental stimulation. Thanks to Gailene Stock, Director of The Australian Ballet School – which, ironically, is the official school of The Australian Ballet – I was hired to choreograph a ballet based on *The Red Shoes*, and I threw myself into it. Being in the studio and working was my safe place; it allowed me to lose myself and the work flowed. Those rehearsal hours gave me courage. I was doing what I was good at for at least a few hours of the day. I felt less vulnerable.

* * *

During this time Michael's condition was worsening. He was afraid, and aware that the AIDS virus was galloping through his body. In fact, we were all afraid; so little was known about the condition, and rumours that AIDS could be spread through casual contact were causing worldwide panic and condemning and demonising the gay community. Being so far away from Michael played on my mind. I needed to be with him. David was aware of my concerns for Michael's vulnerability for, without family support, he was relying on frightened, wary friends. His situation was dire and fragile. And, even though I would miss David and also miss working in the studio, we decided I should go to London to live with Michael and care for him.

With David's support, I boarded a flight for London. I'd planned to read up on the AIDS virus during my flight. All I knew at that time was that the condition was terminal; there was no cure, and it was highly transmissible. Yet I felt strangely protected from the threat of catching AIDS from Michael, even though others expressed fear that, by being with him, my life might well be in danger. But, for me, the thought of Michael dying infused me with strength and the desire to keep him alive.

I arrived in Islington, to the house we had shared. From the outside it looked the same, but nothing prepared me for the sight that stood before me when Michael opened the door. Good looking Michael had withered. His beautiful, blonde locks were thin and dank, the white, straight teeth I'd envied had yellowed. His generous smile was tight, and

I could see fear and panic in his eyes. He ushered me inside, then walked unsteadily to the kitchen to put the kettle on. When he looked back at me, his sad face was streaming with tears, which trickled onto his red t-shirt, leaving dots down the front. With spiky, thin fingers he brushed his face and whispered, "Thanks for coming Bloss." Bloss, his shorthand for Blossom, with a nod to "Petal", is what Michael had always called me. That affectionate nickname stirred so many memories for me. I still had not spoken. I was frozen with the realisation that Michael was so severely diminished; he was fading and frighteningly frail. In contrast, behind his tears, the steely Michael gaze was present, as he struggled to stay calm. For some time we simply looked at each other. There were no words. I did not recognise the haunted expression on Michael's face—an expression I would come to know and fear in other men, over the years, again and again. Michael opened his arms wide. I remember walking into them, soothed by his warm, familiar smell and the particular way he had of holding me as I sobbed deep into his neck.

The house was much the same as I remembered it: toasty warm (a rare luxury in those days), with books everywhere, and walls lined with Michael's artwork and objects d'art randomly placed here and there. Michael's humour and quick wit had endowed him with a knack for creating a wholly original, intriguing home. Looking around it, I recalled how our friends during the '70s had gravitated to 176, as it was known back then, when we were making the most of swinging London. What a carefree time that had been as we costumed ourselves in copycat Twiggy outfits from Mary Quant and Biba, the latter being Barbara Hulanicki's fashion mecca, which eventually made its home on Kensington High Street and boasted the famous Rainbow restaurant and hangout for rock stars and devoted followers of fashion. The house in Islington had been a gathering place, especially during summer, when the rooftop sun deck provided an ideal sun trap during the day and a talking space well into London's long summer evenings. Copious amounts of wine and beer had sparked conversations of dreams and plans, which during those times frequently became a reality. The world had seemed a place of possibility and promise back then, and Michael – with his hilarious sense of humour – had been the entertainer. Some couldn't get enough of him; I was one of them. He was a kind human being blessed with a steel trap mind and a wonderfully contagious laugh. Life was full of expectation... and then came AIDS.

* * *

176 New North Road was a Victorian terrace arranged on four floors with lots of stairs. Once I'd settled in, I suggested Michael move down to the ground floor, as his respiratory system was weak and showing signs of strain when he climbed the stairs to his second-floor bedroom. At first, he was reluctant to move. He said it felt like giving in and, no matter what, he had a life to live. Michael's mantra was that while he had breath, he was alive and intended to stay that way. From his Winnipeg days as a practising Buddhist, he chanted every day; it was his way of finding momentary peace. Listening to his chanting as I cared for the house also brought peace to me, for I knew that his stress and fears would subside for a time, and he'd find a place of respite, which God knows he needed.

Health remedies, potions and lotions filled the kitchen, along with his AZT and numerous other experimental drugs. Before long, more tubs and bottles of medication overwhelmed the house, as Michael was always searching desperately to find something new that might extend his life.

Horrendous side effects from the drugs became a daily problem. Every day new lesions would surface on what was left of his ravaged body. Food was always an issue; no matter how much he ate the weight kept falling away. Friends kindly called before dropping by; they were welcome, as Michael the communicator loved company and, amazingly, was still able to entertain. Hearing their laughter coming from Michael's bedroom or the lounge room gave me momentary strength.

As weeks passed, friends came less and less as the reality of Michael's decline became increasingly painful. I had become accustomed to Michael's frail state; helping him dress and shower became harsh, daily reminders of his weight loss. Once or twice a week we visited the Kobler Outpatient Clinic, which is part of the Chelsea and Westminster hospital on Fulham Road and was the earliest specialist centre for HIV care in the UK. The Kobler Clinic was a godsend for AIDS patients, but it was also a tragic place, with gaunt faces pleading for answers, skeletal arms attached to blood bags. Michael's doctor, Dr Mike Youle, was a young chap dedicated to treating this new disease. He was one of the clinic's founders and served as its Clinical Trials Coordinator. He was also a consultant for the world's global programme on AIDS in Kampala, and had been Director of HIV clinical research at the Royal Free Hospital in London. We were in good hands. Michael adored him, had huge faith in him and was convinced Mike was going to find a cure for this dreaded virus. He loved reminding me how he fancied Dr Mike, adding that it was almost worth getting the virus to have Dr Mike gaze down at him. Michael could get away with saying something like that and we'd dissolve into shrieks of laughter.

But of course, Dr Mike could find no cure. No one could. As time went on, blood transfusions were becoming a regular occurrence, and what a difference they made to

Michael's general well-being, even if the benefits were short lived. His T-cells were constantly falling, and he was showing signs of a diarrheal illness called cryptosporidiosis, caused by a parasite which attacks people suffering from the AIDS virus and others with a weakened immune system. Because of it, he was spending more time heading to the toilet than doing anything else. We were usually awakened two or three times a night as he suffered stomach pain and needed the bathroom. Fortunately for us, Dr Mike was available to give him support and help throughout the night and day.

There came a point when Michael was too exhausted to entertain friends, which meant, more often than not, it was just us at home. We were cocooned in the house, talking about old times, laughing a lot, and sometimes sharing tears. This was a time when the virus was gaining force throughout the world, with deaths rising and rumours about contamination never ceasing. TV warnings bombarded every home with the gruesome message: the Grim Reaper is coming to get you. Travel abroad was severely restricted for those with the virus—a constraint that would last for 20 years. The stigma attached to AIDS was brutal; many lost jobs, others were abandoned by their family and thrown onto the street. Anger and disgust hurled at the gay population became the norm. Any person who appeared to be gay faced mockery and exclusion. As general opinion held that the virus had been started by gay men, it quickly became known as the "Gay Disease", and the hatred unleashed caused the gay population to hide in fear of their lives.

Weeks passed without my noticing the days passing by. Michael needed endless care, assistance and emotional support every minute of the day. I forgot the time, date or month as our days merged into each other, followed by dreaded sleepless nights. I was feeling scattered, dashing every which way, looking for relief—any escape that would shield me from having to acknowledge what was going to happen. I knew I could not abandon Michael, I had to hold on despite the terrifying fear that would creep over me. There was no way out, no place to run. I knew I was going to watch Michael die. How would that be, I wondered, and could I do it?

My thoughts would veer back to when I was a child and constantly worried that my mother would die. I remembered how I imagined that one day I'd come home from school and she would have gone, or be somewhere in the house dead. This fear was so intense that I'd call her during my lunch hour from the coin box on the corner to be sure she was alive. It was horrible, that fear. I know now that the reason I experienced such a dread of loss and abandonment stemmed from my mother's constant refrain that she wanted to sail far away and never come back. She repeated those words so often they eventually became meaningless to me, devoid of power. Only when faced with the severity of Michael's condition did the terror of abandonment her words had engendered surface again to haunt me.

* * *

I knew Michael's death was upon us. Every day was filled with more signs of the virus progressing. The Kaposi sarcoma lesions were digging into the little flesh Michael had left on his body; they were everywhere. Pain would come and go, and sleep disappeared for us both. We didn't want to sleep. Time was running out, and every single moment was one I wanted to hold on to and not let go. Michael clung to his life, speaking of the future, planning driving lessons. His relentless positivity helped me cope, as did his quick sense of humour, which would spring out of nowhere even during the grimmest of times. I never really knew if Michael truly believed he would come out of this or if he was simply protecting us both from the inevitable. I rather think it was the latter.

Michael's daily needs mounted; there was endless washing of bed linen due to his uncontrollable diarrhoea, and there was the searching for food that he could keep down and would not hurt his badly ulcerated mouth. It all had to be done. Yet he was becoming more and more withered every day. One night, pain thrashed through Michael's body with unrelenting force. I called the Kobler Centre who advised I get Michael to Mildmay Mission Hospice in Hackney the following day. That night was endless, but somewhere within my bones I knew exactly what I had to do. During the early hours of the morning, probably due to lack of sleep, I felt as though a demon had descended upon us. I remember very clearly, as I watched dawn break, my determination, against Michael's wishes, to get him into a taxi as quickly as possible and deliver him to Mildmay Mission Hospice.

As we approached the check-in desk the receptionist's expression told me all I needed to know. There was no booking for Michael Manning Brown, and they had no spare beds. At this point Michael caved in. He was shattered physically and mentally. Someone eventually arrived with a wheelchair for Michael, and I turned into what must have looked like a demented devil woman, telling the receptionist over and over that we would not leave the building, and that they had to help us. I do not recall how long this went on, but obviously the staff realised I was worn ragged, and Michael was close to death. Eventually, a bed in a quiet room was found.

Although the word hospice was never spoken between us, it hung in the air, declaring we had arrived at the last resort, a place Michael did not want to visit. Once we'd settled in, the staff took over, giving us time to rest and rekindle. Medication brought relief to most of Michael's pain. The staff bestowed endless care and affection upon him. He'd make them laugh, which they loved; his laughter spoke volumes. He'd captured their hearts, and often they would pop in just to spend time with us. He had not lost his magic. And, even in the depths of this hellhole, Michael never failed to thank the staff for their patience and kindness. I don't recall seeing our doctor Mike ever again once we went into the hospice.

The staff made a bed for me beside Michael; they knew this wife was not to be moved. We were safe, help was at hand, our life was as comfortable as it could be. With the palliative team taking over we were left to share the precious moments we had left. Michael's needs were escalating. With his wonderful nurses attending non-stop to bouts of dry-retching, diarrhoea, bedsore dressings, medications, changing bed linen, adjusting pain relief, turning Michael's fragile body as well as bringing food for me, it felt as though we were on a fast-track treadmill that was not going to stop.

My niece Carina arrived from Australia, bringing her special kind of worldliness and quiet empathy; qualities she has always had. Carina had a deep closeness with Uncle Michael; he'd played a large part in her growing up, and later as an adult when she was working in London and staying in our home at 176. From a very early age she grasped his wit, happily responding and egging him on to dish out more outrageous pranks and fun talk. Due to family commitments in Australia she left before Michael died. Saying goodbye to her Uncle Michael tore her up. She was heartbroken.

Towards the end of two and a half weeks in the hospice, Michael was still holding on tightly to his life, fighting every day. Often, he'd simply gaze into my eyes. Then one day suddenly he said, "Bloss, there are a few pennies in my bank account. Buy something lovely for yourself. I've loved you every minute of every day since the moment we met that warm, fun day on Earl's Court Road, you in your mini skirt and your long black hair."

Those were his last words to me.

Soon after that, late at night, he very slowly turned his head away from me, something he'd never done before. I knew instantly that he had died.

I held Michael for the longest time until the staff came to wash him. I helped them damp down his wafer-thin body. Bones draped in skin were all that was left.

When we'd left the house for the last time, a few weeks before, I'd dressed Michael in his favourite red trainers, his navy-blue sweater, cap and scarf. They were still where I'd put them, in the drawer by his bed, so I got them out and, very carefully, with the help of his favourite nurse, I dressed him. He'd have liked that. Then they took him away. For some time, I stayed on his bed.

* * *

The house was empty when I arrived back, scattered with signs of a hasty departure, coffee cups, medication jars, unmade beds, a sad mess. Nothing made sense. I needed rest and sleep. When I awoke, I knew I had some major things left to do for Michael and threw myself into sorting his funeral. Michael had no family and mine were in Australia, so a friend accompanied me to the local funeral parlour. I got through the legal steps registering Michael's death, contacting friends and the Buddhist Centre. It turned out that Michael had told the monks that he wanted a Buddhist funeral. This was news, as Michael had never even mentioned dying to me. However, I believed them; I just knew it to be true. The service was conducted by the monks. No speaking, no fuss, just an outpouring of love. Many of our friends turned up. I was happy to see them and feel the love they had for Michael and the warmth they shed upon me.

* * *

Days passed. In time I cleared the house and rented it out to lovely dancers who were working at Sadler's Wells Theatre not far away. During the clean out I reached a point of sheer exhaustion, not knowing how I was going to keep going. It was then that there was a knock at the door, two young people arrived saying they had been sent to help me. They were volunteers from the AIDS charity the Terrence Higgins Trust, and were the first angels who would appear just when I felt unable to go on. They mucked in, working all day packing and lugging boxes, washing the floors and shopping for food. Their kindness broke me; I shed grateful tears when we parted.

A day later I collected Michael's ashes and carried them around in my shopping bag for days, unable to let go of them. They comforted me. I wanted to be sure they were safe. This was a private act. No one knew I had Michael's ashes with me but, somehow, I gained courage just keeping what was left of him in my care.

After a few weeks of sorting the house, I knew I had to leave London and decided to place Michael's ashes in the garden by the back wall, and there they stayed for the following 30 years until I sold the house in 2021. No one knew that was where Michael's ashes were. He'd loved the house and the garden, and it seemed the best place for him to rest. I'd taken a small amount to keep with me, which of course I have kept.

Years before, when we'd danced in Winnipeg, Michael had taken many reels of 16-millimetre film and later put them on a CD for me. I still look at it during those moments when I feel the need to see him.

* * *

David and I had been constantly in touch while I was in London, his quiet support always in the background. He knew from the start of our relationship that I would always love Michael. I remember once telling David that my ideal life would be to live in a house with David, next door to Michael. David had no problem with that statement; he never felt threatened by my love for Michael, which made David all the more lovable to me.

When I was ready to leave London, David was in New York dancing with The Australian Ballet at the Metropolitan Opera House, so I flew there to spend time with him on my way back to Australia. Leaving Heathrow, my guardian angel appeared for the second time. I was flying Pan American economy, patiently waiting my turn to check in, feeling composed with the thought that, for this moment, I was just like everyone else. I felt orderly, my armour firmly in place. I was sure no one could possibly suspect how miserable, exhausted and stressed I was when, without warning, uncontrolled tears started flowing down my face and would not stop. My insides were throbbing. I was hurting so much and ashamed that my cover up was breaking down and I was caving in for all to see. I remember being taken out of the queue by a woman, who brought me to a place in the terminal where we sat for some time. The conversation fails me now, but the next thing I knew she was escorting me onto the aircraft and when we turned into business class, she sat me down and left. I'd been rescued by a kind person who just knew help was required.

When I arrived in New York David was gentle, aware of my weakened body and mind. The company were staying at the Mayflower Hotel on Central Park West, close to the Metropolitan Opera House. We'd stayed at the Mayflower before as it was a favourite haunt of dancers and artists. The ballet company greeted me warmly.

Performing in New York was a huge deal for The Australian Ballet. However, I was suffering from battle fatigue and no amount of good will, or even my love for David, could endow me with the energy I would have needed to front up at the Opera House. David never questioned or minded that I didn't see his New York performances. He was a big thinker, never needy, and the one least likely to require performance affirmation. I spent time walking the huge avenues of New York and lolling about in Central Park, which in those days was not the safest place in which to languish. But the vibe always felt good in New York, and I allowed myself to marinate in it. After spending a few days in Washington, I took a flight back to Melbourne. I needed to be there.

* * *

Our graceful home wrapped its arms around me. I felt safe. The house hung on the slope of a hillside with panoramic views throughout the entire house of the nature reserve below. All year long, sunshine filled every room from 11am until sunset. Long walks in our nature reserve were accompanied by my wise and kind friend Judy Waterhouse, who helped me to absorb and accept all that had happened. Judy listened. She never judged, which made me feel free to think out loud without censoring any thoughts or emotions. At times she'd respond with gentle humour, and I'd end up laughing at myself. All of this was a special gift Judy bestowed on me during that difficult time—a gift for which I am forever grateful.

I loved living in our house, though originally I had wanted a Victorian terrace, thinking to set up a London-style home in Australia. David was not to be persuaded. Having spent his entire life in cold, dark Victorian houses he could only think of open, spacious living. He had his heart set on an Australian house consisting of four bedrooms and a view, a swimming pool, a large garden and sunlight throughout. The house he chose had been built by a local architect in the late '60s. It had come with brown and orange tiled bathroom and kitchen, and floor-length turquoise curtains that fell from teak pelmets. Over the years some decorating took place, but we got used to the quirkiness.

**

David arrived back from the American tour and our life resumed. I'd started to enjoy the laugh of kookaburras who gathered in the big eucalyptus trees at the foot of our garden, which led directly into the Keilor Nature Reserve. That summer, a mother duck decided to hatch her ducklings in our garden and teach them to swim in our pool. David was not happy about her taking over our pool, as their presence upset the chemicals, which then required constant adjusting. Nevertheless, in spite of the inconvenience, there they stayed, tiny ducks learning to swim. One morning the mother duck stood by the edge of the pool, quacking loudly. It turned out that her ducklings, during their first swimming lessons, were too tiny to get themselves out of the pool as the sides were too high for the ducklings to climb. They were panicking and after we'd dashed downstairs David quietly slipped into the pool and lifted each one out, placing them gently at the webbed feet of their mum who was anxiously waiting by the pool's edge. David then put his building skills to use and erected a plank covered in a towel which would stop their little feet from slipping so the tiny things could scramble up on their own. This mother duck was a great mum; not only did she show her babes how to waddle up the plank but there she sat by the pool calling to them, quacking away until each one managed to make it to dry land. We loved their presence and enjoyed the many weeks they stayed with us. The gift was that this happened every year for the following five years. Each year the mother duck would arrive, find her nesting spot in the garden and, when her babes were ready, the swimming lessons would commence overseen by her tender loving care. We developed a friendly arrangement, looking forward to her arrival each year.

* * *

Life in Melbourne was comfortable, and the next few years were productive for me. I opened a local ballet school, staged *The Snow Queen* for The Australian Ballet School and continued working on my full-length ballet *The Red Shoes*. Both ballets worked well and were revived many times over the years. *The Red Shoes* entered the repertoire of Singapore Ballet, *The Snow Queen* was performed by Hong Kong Ballet, and it would become The Australian Ballet School's signature work. David and I were given a Cavalier King Charles puppy who quickly took over our lives, demanding walks in the nature reserve and travelling to Sydney with me when I'd joined David, who would be performing with The Australian Ballet at the Sydney Opera House.

Over the preceding three years, small imperfections had begun to seep into David's dancing. I doubt they were perceptible to his audiences, but he saw them, and had no doubt as to what they foretold. These imperfections were stubbornly immune to correction, causing less assurance in David's dancing during both rehearsal and performance. His body had started to have a mind of its own, no longer responding as it always had. The fine detail of his cut-glass classical technique, something he was known for, was fudging. Bit by bit, the cracks were showing. His buoyant elevation was lost. No amount of rehearsal was going to restore the ease and clarity of his natural technique.

As he became increasing aware that the inevitable was in sight, I recognised his anticipatory grief. It was all around him, free floating, hanging in the air. There were no words. There didn't need to be. We both knew that soon he was going to have to part from his greatest love. I'd seen that same bleak look on Rudolf Nureyev's face when he toured Australia, teetering on the very edge of his dancing days, hoping he could make it through a performance.

As I walked into the Sydney Opera House one Saturday, quite close to curtain up time, I bumped into some of the dancers who casually said, "If you're looking for David he's just left." Alarm bells rang; I'd come to see a performance in which David was to be dancing. On hearing he'd left the theatre I immediately took the ferry back to Manly Beach where we were staying. David was on the balcony, gazing out at the ocean. His restrained body language told me all I needed to know. What he'd been processing for some time had led him, on this night, before that performance, to where it had inevitably been leading him. Much later that night we shared a bottle of wine while sitting by the sea. There was nothing to discuss. David had closed the door, leaving behind his lifelong addiction and passion.

The company were keen to throw a farewell performance party, which is the norm when a principal dancer retires. David was adamant that this would not happen. There was to be no commotion, no sentimental speeches, no hullabaloo. It was heart-wrenching to see him struggling and drowning in massive grief. Unlike me, he never wanted to discuss ballet and certainly, once retired, he would not watch performances. Until I knew better, I'd try to coax him to attend performances where he could be on the lookout for new potential. His reply was always the same. "I don't want to talk about ballet or watch it. My thirst for ballet is only quenched by the sensation of doing it."

David was in mourning. Ballet was sacred to him. The stage was, for him, a place of intimacy and, beyond that, a place he owned—where he was completely comfortable and lost in the process of portraying a character, of moving, turning, leaping and being the essence of grace and chivalry when partnering his ballerina. Though many people he encountered perceived him as emotionally unavailable, on the stage he was able to express the deepest and grandest emotions, unhindered, at will. He could take you where he wanted to take you and, in the absence of that outlet, he would be bereft for the rest of his life. I think I knew, even on the night when we sat together on the beach, that he would never manage to replace what dancing had meant to him. And he never did. He knew he couldn't, so he didn't try. Once he walked away from dancing he was never the same again.

* * *

There followed a difficult time of adjustment for David, as he tried his best to move on. He became an excellent tennis player, working with a coach and participating in competitions at our local club. True to his established ways it was not enough to play on the weekend; weeknights became crammed with tennis matches and competitions, though he liked the weekend matches particularly. He was always seeking to better his game, seeking perfection.

Although I had learned to play tennis well at school, I did not enjoy competition tennis. The earnest approach required took the joy out of the game for me. I recall one occasion when David asked if I'd fill in when another player called in sick. As it was an outdoor, night-time match on a rather cool evening I very reluctantly agreed, after much pleading from David. During the pre-match chit chat David casually announced, "This is Petal. She's agreed to help out tonight."

I was playing against David and as we sauntered onto the court one of the women whose team I was on quietly said, "Keep an eye on David, he's got white line fever. He plays to win."

"I know," I replied. "I'm his wife."

We hooted with laughter causing David to glare across the court at us with his most frosty English expression. I teased him on the way home, saying my team won because I was on it, so perhaps I should consider joining up. Quick to reply, David said membership was at full capacity, but that he'd think about shortlisting me once my game improved, and we laughed and continued to tease each other all the way home.

Still, it was all too clear to me that the distractions he devised never really worked; they came and went. There were hours spent cutting and pruning our lovely garden, cataloguing his Moorcroft pottery collection, swimming 60 laps a day in our pool – which made him wonderfully fit – and writing every evening a daily account of his day's activities. These things helped a bit, but he was still hurting and was often unavailable emotionally. I knew better than to prod and poke at him. This pain was something he needed to deal with in his own way.

He'd always had a strong desire to see much of Australia, especially the outback. One night he announced to me that he'd been chatting to a chap who suggested he obtain a heavy-duty truck licence so he'd be able to drive through and experience the fierceness of the outback. Big rigs fascinated David; he'd always been a petrol head, buying car after car.

But when he told me this new, rather quixotic plan, I was inwardly shattered, thinking *good God, too dangerous, too lonely*. Yet for David it was no more nor less than a huge, much-needed challenge and, six months later, after two failed attempts, he passed his test and off he went, loving every aspect. I gave him as much encouragement as I could muster but I was scared stiff of this adventure.

He drove into the heart of Australia on several occasions, always with an experienced buddy driver there for support. It proved to be a dangerous game, requiring nerves of steel and no fear of Australia's vast, unforgiving centre. So, while the alien landscape excited and intrigued him, it became clear to him that holding one's nerve while manoeuvring a massive trailer through rough terrain is a young man's job. He simply did not have the brute strength required to handle that massive equipment, and though he loved the challenge and the freedom, having to execute up to 18 gears became more and more daunting. He also came to realise that many drivers were born into the heavy-duty driving game, learning the drill when it was handed down through their families. David loved the ride but had to admit that, for him, it was not destined to be a lengthy endeavour.

In need of something to fill his time, he began teaching ballet, passing on his dancing knowledge and experience. He was good at it, as I knew he would be. Dancers loved working with him and were attracted to his quiet way of sharing what he knew. He was always gracious and patient and kind, never imposing or insisting his way was best. He'd let the dancers explore, gently showing the way when needed. I knew this beautiful man was doing his best to find another absorption, another love, but there remained about him a lingering wistfulness. And the truth is that, while teaching gave him something to do, his heart was never in it. He was not driven to do it, and it could never replace what he'd had.

So much loss: our baby, Michael's death, my job, David's career. I was often struggling. I seemed to have enough to occupy my days, though I found myself longing for the spontaneity of London and all that it offers. But I had responsibilities to tend to. My parents were in their mid-90s by this time and, while both were in sound mind, things had become worrying. My father was diagnosed with macular degeneration when he was 70 and lost his sight fairly quickly—yet he still insisted on using public transport, travelling alone as he navigated his way across Perth to the School for the Blind. He would do this until he reached the age of 94. He appeared fearless. Protective of retaining his independence and confidence, he attended woodwork classes that the school provided.

I visited my parents as often as I could, and it was apparent that they were starting to need full-time assistance. They had spent the previous 12 years living in a gentle retirement community in a peaceful suburb on the edge of the Perth. The Retirement Village, as it was known, had three categories: independent living; semi-independent living; nursing home full care. My dashing from Melbourne to Perth became a necessity as their tiny accommodation was becoming cluttered and their personal clothing needed frequent replacing and dry cleaning. General washing of linen and towels was taken care of by the nursing home, but attending to their small personal needs required my attention. As I had been given power of attorney for my parents I was also taking care of their finances, which they could no longer fathom. My darling father found it painful to hand over his bank accounts to me, as did my mother when she was no longer capable of looking after her handbag. I was as careful and respectful as I could be with them, thinking how very much I would hate to hand over my personal life to the care of another.

I could see that they were no longer coping, and I feared that, due to their frailness, danger lurked. I arranged an assessment, which recommended they receive full-time support and that a move to the nursing home should be implemented. I was convinced it would be the safest place for them. But my mother, with her sharp mindedness and mischievous twinkle, and my father, with his sweet-natured patience and consideration for everyone, were not buying it.

I understood their fear of the nursing home. It would mean that, after 60 years of married life, they would live on different wards. The thought of separating them was deeply painful for me and I understood that it would be unbearable for them. No amount of persuasion from me would induce the head of staff to change the system, which decreed men on one floor, women on another. Of course, I understood that most people don't make it into a nursing home together as usually one or the other has died. But in this case my parents were both alive, of sound mind and – most significantly – still very much in love. I spoke gently to them, saying the move was essential for their safety. I also told them, as kindly and frankly as possible, that knowing they were safe would relieve me of the stress I felt regarding their care. The last thing they wanted was for me to be plagued with concern for them so, with all the love in the world, they agreed to go into the nursing home, knowing full well what lay ahead. I will never forget the morning I delivered them to their separate wards. My heart ached as, other than necessary separations when my mother was in hospital, my parents had spent every night of their married life together.

It was a brutal act. But my dear father managed to see his sweetheart every day. He'd sit with her and remind her that the move was for the best. I found it all horribly painful, and when my father whispered to me one morning that he'd decided he was not going to do this for much longer I told him I understood. He died a few weeks later. My mother was broken-hearted. She cried and cried for him. Shortly after his death the school for the blind wrote to me praising his courage and acknowledging the inspiration and role model he'd become to others at the school. I was not surprised; this was a man I knew well and loved. My dad. Staff at the nursing home had constantly told me what a dear man he was; they said they would do anything for him. On hearing this I would glow, agreeing with them wholeheartedly. I suppose because my parents were in their 40s when they had me he was more of a grandfather to me. I remember cuddling into him... to this day I miss him.

After his death, my mother's life at the nursing home became unbearable. The staff were rude and disrespectful. She made it clear to them that she was proud that I had been a ballet dancer and had given her nice presents of nightdresses and jumpers bought from around the world, and that each present had come with a story of where I was when I bought it for her. Apparently, this annoyed the staff, but that didn't keep my mother from mentioning it. I can only imagine her pleasure in reminding them that she was cared for and spoilt by her globe-trotting ballet dancer daughter. The staff were also aware that her mind was razor sharp, free from any sign of dementia. She was well mannered, eloquent, up to date with world affairs and happy to converse on many subjects, including her beloved music and art. She asked not to be referred to by her first name, Marjorie, preferring to be addressed as Mrs Miller, which in my mind was a reasonable request from a woman in her early 90s. My feeling is that they perceived her as being beyond her station, and hence took delight in referring to her as The Dame. But my mother didn't suffer slights or fools lightly, and she knew when they were nastily sending her up. On one occasion, I arrived to find her with a large black eye; one of the staff who really disliked her threw her bell at her and hit her in the face. I was astonished, as I also was when they said she had sprained her ankle. This did not make sense as my mother had been bed-ridden for some time.

As the weeks and months passed, she was gradually becoming less aware and more unsure of things. She had been a spirited woman when she entered the nursing home. Eighteen months later, given the ill treatment she received there, coupled with the death of her beloved husband, there was not much left. I spent a great deal of time with her, but it was impossible for me to be there on a permanent basis, which I deeply regret. I protected her as much as I could; it was not enough. And I had to be careful not to rock the boat—calling out the people who treated her so poorly would, I was sure, only have the effect of them disliking her and damaging her even more.

David knew I was working hard to keep my head above water. One night over dinner he suggested I take a trip to London; he felt a change would uplift me, and he knew London could do that for me, as it had become my spiritual home. I relished the thought of being completely at ease in that huge city, knowing endless options were at my fingertips. Just thinking about it improved my mood. I booked a flight, intending to stay only a couple of weeks.

* * *

While I was in London, Gailene Stock, who'd recently been appointed Director of The Royal Ballet School, offered me a teaching position there. I was flattered by the offer, but did not entertain it for a moment. I had committed to a life in Australia. Melbourne was my home; return I must. Gailene then asked if I would visit White Lodge, which is The Royal Ballet School's junior boarding school, and look at classes nine and eleven.

She wanted my opinion on the talent. Students are accepted into the school at age 11 and commence full-time ballet training for a period of five years, after which they graduate to the Upper School in Covent Garden for a further three years. In all my years as a dancer in the company I had never visited White Lodge, and I was curious about it. So I agreed to Gailene's request to spend a day there.

White Lodge is a Grade I listed Georgian house, which lies at the heart of London's magnificent Richmond Park. With an illustrious history as a former royal hunting lodge, and occupants including King George II, Queen Victoria and the baby Queen Elizabeth II, it remains part of the Crown Estate to this day. Driving though Richmond Park I was mesmerised by the tranquillity of the grounds and the herds of deer mulling about in the summer sun. When I'd joined Sadler's Wells Royal Ballet at age 25, I encountered many dancers who'd come through White Lodge and spoke incessantly about their days as boarders there. I had found it odd that they had been so sheltered and spoke of little else.

On arriving at White Lodge, I was greeted by the Ballet Principal, Mary Goodhew, a graceful blonde woman with a charming English accent. I'd known Mary when we were both dancers in Sadler's Wells Royal Ballet. She gave me a tour of the Lodge followed by morning tea in her elegant office. She explained the history of White Lodge, after which we moved to the Nelson Room, which is where Lord Horatio Nelson dined in 1805 and set out his plan for the Battle of Trafalgar, illustrating it by drawing on a table top with a wine-moistened finger. One hundred and fifty years later, in 1955, the lease for White Lodge became available and was granted to Sadler's Wells Ballet School for 150 girls and "a few boys" to board. A year later it became The Royal Ballet School, with Princess Margaret as its President. The grand public opening, in 1957, was presided over by Dame Margot Fonteyn.

Little gems of interest popped up at every corner: a life-sized bronze statue of Margot Fonteyn graced the entrance hall, along with a dressing table that had belonged to Anna Pavlova. Mary saved the Salon studio to last; a prize worth waiting for. Before me were long windows and doors looking out down a flight of stairs to Queen Charlotte's drive. The room had a warm glow about it. It was painted yellow, with chandeliers above and vintage photographs of the Royal Family everywhere. A ballet barre flanked the room, and a large, gilt-edged mirror occupied one entire wall. In the corner sat a grand piano. I was transported by this place of quiet gentleness oozing with royal heritage and ballet history. Mary was right when she'd said we were on hallowed ground.

Eventually, Mary ushered me to the ballet studios. There they were: a roomful of perfectly proportioned little bodies, wide-eyed and eager, each one engrossed in their barre work. As we entered, the teacher stopped the class, at which point the young dancers turned to us and gracefully executed a formal ballet reverence accompanied by the pianist. I was touched and charmed by this formal gesture used by the school to welcome guests.

As the afternoon progressed, I could feel I was being sucked in. Each young dancer demonstrated perfect technique for their level, as well as musicality, focus and expressiveness. I was smitten. How was I going to address this opportunity? I knew I'd been thrown a lifeline. My instinct was telling me, *go home, do not disrupt your life, leave now*, but then a booming voice inside my head declared *you know you want to be here*.

Driving out of Richmond Park that afternoon I felt more alive than I'd felt for a long time. Just for an afternoon I was back with my tribe, where I belonged. I was at ease, free from the uncomfortable feelings I'd been living with. I called

David, told him about the day and the offer. His reply was instant. "Do it," he said. The next morning I met with Gailene Stock to inform her that I'd be happy to accept her offer for one year. Gailene looked right chuffed with herself saying, "I knew, if I could get you to see the year nine girls, I'd get you in."

* * *

Leaving Australia was right for me. I needed to heal from the past few years. I knew my mother was frail but not close to death. I was deeply uneasy about leaving her to the mercy of the nursing home staff but, if necessary, I could and would hop on a plane. The thought of working again at the highest level pushed me through my concerns. I had been asked to train the most valued ballet potential in the Western world. I needed to grab the opportunity and run with it.

David's staunch support made the move much easier. Fifteen years of working and living together had cemented our relationship. We were two individuals who understood the other's need for growth and space. Neither David nor I could have tolerated being controlled by the other; we relished our differences. I knew our bond provided the assurance we both needed when apart. Not having children did have the benefit of allowing us uninterrupted time together and had kept our intimacy intact, which we cherished.

Within days, I knew I'd made the right decision in leaving Australia, at least for a while. Connecting with friends and visiting galleries had lightened my thoughts, while working in the studio with the students filled me with renewed strength. I couldn't get enough of it. I knew that Gailene felt strongly that being a professional dancer was not essential to becoming a ballet teacher, although she regarded stage experience as an added advantage. She insisted that her teachers have many years of practical studio teaching, and that a studied knowledge of anatomy was essential for instructing classical ballet technique. She also recognised that teaching ballet to gifted students is a massive responsibility, but that dedicated teachers thrive on the daily demands. Ballet training is repetitive. The daily, detailed lessons are constantly repeated. The ballet syllabus is rigid and requires dedication and commitment from both student and teacher.

* * *

Having joined the teaching staff at White Lodge, every morning before my classes I'd retreat to the gorgeous Salon, to prepare my body and mind for my day ahead. The Salon offered me some moments of silence, which I needed. Here, there were no students chatting, no tinkling of the piano, no anxious teachers checking up on classes. It was a space that struck me as untroubled and serene. No doubt the Salon had been a Royal Family gathering spot for formal events, a place where royalty could take in the glorious view of Queen Charlotte Drive beyond the grand French doors. As I flexed each muscle while clearing the monkey chatter from my brain, I cherished my private ritual in the Salon. Sometimes my mind would wander, and I'd imagine Queen Charlotte on her stately horse, riding up the long drive to the front of the Lodge.

It was during this time that I made use of the advice Professor Martin Comte had shared with me. He had been my tutor when I was struggling through my Grad Certificate in Visual and Performing Arts, which I'd undertaken at the behest of Gailene Stock who was then Director of The Australian Ballet School, and felt strongly that dance teachers should be encouraged to further their education. The course I took was the brainchild of Professor Comte, a wise man

I respected and admired. During one of my meltdown moments when I considering abandoning the degree I told him, "I'm not an academic, this is too hard."

Professor Comte replied, "Petal you are a born teacher. You may be sorry if you don't see this through." He had voiced and clarified something I knew to be true.

Once in the studio, teaching six hours a day, Professor Comte's ideas were incredibly valuable. He believed that, no matter the difficulties of the day, one must be sure to leave students with positive thoughts: if they're left dangling and downtrodden getting their attention the next day will be harder than need be. He also spoke in depth about establishing the right tone of delivery; something I'd found lacking in many teachers over the years. As the professor noted, any thought or correction relayed in an annoyed or dull way guarantees the message will be discounted or lost. Teaching with enthusiasm and humour and encouraging students to participate verbally was the goal—one that really worked for me. I had no doubt that love, humour, nurturing and endless patience comprise the formula required to allow students to ripen and unfold. As I put all of this into practice, I was on a roll. Driving to Richmond Park each morning from Shepherd's Bush became my thinking time, during which I'd ruminate on my students' progress and consider ways I could take them further without pressure. The responsibility that came with nurturing their talent was something I greatly enjoyed. I was mindful of not flooding them with information they were not yet able to absorb.

On Sundays, I found it impossible not to wander over to the house in Islington. I wanted to reassure myself that I was okay when thinking about the time Michael and I had there, and that I could be there without falling apart. The ballet dancer tenants to whom I'd rented were lovely; they took extra care of the house. Each time I visited for maintenance reasons I'd wander to the back of the garden where I'd placed Michael's ashes. I came to love those private moments.

I missed him.

* * *

My year of teaching at White Lodge quickly came to an end. Without hesitation, I decided to extend my contract for one more year. I was healing, doing what I loved, what I was good at and taking great enjoyment in supporting my students. The gap in my life was filling up and I was nourished by the understanding that my contribution to these students would not be wasted. They were like sponges, eager for every bit of information and experience they could squeeze out of me on a daily basis. If I had been drowning before, now I was coming up for air.

As I was going to remain in London, David secured a teaching position with London Studio Centre. We closed our home in Melbourne, knowing we'd have a lovely nest to retire to when the time came. I realised I'd left one life and entered another. I was at ease with myself and my work; all else seemed to dilute and leave me in peace. I spoke to my mother twice a week by phone; she seemed to be coping with the nursing home, and I could tell that it gave her joy to know I was happy doing what I loved.

* * *

My life with David often seemed extreme, as we swung from sorrow and pain to getting back on track to start all over again. We managed always to find time for ourselves, curling up together with a DVD, sharing a top drop of champagne, reminiscing about how, back in the '70s, we'd treat ourselves to a bottle of Mateus Rosé on the weekend.

David's great love, other than being on the stage, was his Moorcroft pottery collection. No piece was too small or too broken. His avid collecting had been served well by our touring with ballet companies in the UK and Australia. In each city, local antique, bric-a-brac shops and charity stores were all on the list for a browse. His collection gained momentum, expanding weekly, as did David's knowledge of the heritage of the pottery. It became clear to me David had an addiction; he was a true collector. I was married to a magpie. I took an interest in the collection and enjoyed sharing David's knowledge. We had fun getting hold of a rare piece for a good price. After 40 years, the collection was huge, stored in boxes all over the house that were listed and dated. Favourite pieces were placed about the house until I confessed to him that I felt I was living in a shop. I sometimes struggled with David's accumulating, with his vast collection of ballet and theatre memorabilia, 2000 books on ballet, theatre design and art plus the Moorcroft collection. By 1999 he had amassed more than 300 pieces of Moorcroft. Unlike David I needed open areas; collecting cluttered my head as well as my personal space. However, I knew this was part of our living together, sharing and accommodating each other's quirks. Our intimate life was passionate. It was the bedrock of our togetherness and kept us close each time the random poker fell our way—which it invariably did.

During that year I got a call from the nursing home in Perth saying my mother was poorly and I needed to be there. David rushed me to Heathrow, and I made it to her bedside. We spent three loving days together, during which time I got to know a different woman from the one I had known as my mother. She seemed to separate our relationship from that of mother and daughter to one of woman to woman as she confided deep truths about her younger life. She needed to tell me these things and found comfort in doing so. I promised to keep her past private and safe. The things she told me during those three days left me believing that she had carried shame throughout her life, which may have accounted for her edginess and depression.

One night, overcome with tiredness, I decided to grab some sleep in a nearby room. I awoke to my great niece Lydia telling me my mother had died. She and my niece had popped by to see her late that night, and were with her when she passed away. I was grateful they were there but profoundly sorry I'd not been there for her at the last. Filled with regret, I promised myself that if ever I was in that position again with someone else I loved, I would not leave, no matter how tired I was.

Even though my mother had been in her mid-90s I was not prepared for her death. How does one prepare for the feeling of loss and separation that death engenders? I was going to miss her challenging ways. Despite her physical frailties and her threats of running away that frightened me so when I was a child she was, most significantly a feisty, authentic Australian woman; if you asked her opinion you needed to be sure you were ready for her answer. She was steadfast in her support of me. I will never forget that, when my other relatives were saying I should forget about dancing and become a nurse, it was my mother who told me, "Be a ballerina."

Over the years I'd listened to my parents as they insisted on paying for and sorting in detail their funeral arrangements. These conversations had become a regular feature between us, as they made slight changes to their plans with my father never failing to add, "I won't have you handing the hat around for our funerals, my girl." I was accustomed to these conversations; they were important to my parents if somewhat disturbing to me. One important wish was that they were to be buried in a nature reserve cemetery on the outskirts of Perth.

And they were. The burial sites are shaded by large eucalyptus trees resting among winding grass lawns. The air is filled with the continuous singing of kookaburras, and large, languishing kangaroos appear to be keeping guard. It is a beautiful place to finally rest. My parents had taken care of everything—there was nothing for me to do other than to alert the funeral parlour. The people there were kind, telling me all was attended to other than for me to choose a date for the service and get some rest. I was deeply grateful to my parents. Their meticulous planning was an act of love, and provided a lesson I would come to use later, thus relieving my loved ones of not having to make personal decisions on my behalf once my life had ceased to be. After my mother was laid to rest, there followed the sorting of my parents' belongings. Neither I nor anyone else had use for my mother's precious crystal dishes, or for boxes of stuff gathered during a marriage of 75 years. The charity shop did well.

Even though I'd not lived in Perth since leaving at 18, I had remained firmly attached to my parents. After their deaths I discovered I'd not moved away from them emotionally at all. Not having children of my own and with both parents gone I felt adrift. I was going to have to work hard at living without their unconditional love and support. I will always remember my mother's facial expression whenever we'd meet, and the way it spoke of pride and even disbelief about who she'd given birth to. Her approval empowered me and made me smile.

***

"Your greatest competition is the dancer you know you can be. She's the one you need to worry about."

Choreographer Agnes de Mille to Petal, during her time working with Royal Winnipeg Ballet—words that were to become one of Petal's mantras

Throughout the following ten years, David and I travelled between Australia and London. At Christmas time and during the school holidays we'd happily fly back to our Melbourne home. The arrangement suited us both. In 2000 we'd bought a small flat in Shepherd's Bush, close to all transport, as a lock-up-and-go London pad on the 8th floor of an Art Deco building overlooking West London. The flat was toasty warm and trouble free. The area was multicultural, a colourful cross-section of languages sang out, often late at night, and sari-clad women shopped in the famous Shepherd's Bush market, which sold every conceivable fruit and veg. Posh Holland Park Road, where the very rich and extremely famous bought grand houses, was only a four-minute walk across Shepherd's Bush Green roundabout. We made the most of London life. Work provided the creative nourishment we needed, and the family gaps in our lives were filled with other people's children whom we taught and mentored.

During this time David would have happily lived in Australia. He'd developed a true love for the country and its people. His joy was his year-round seasonal kit of shorts, t-shirt and flip flops or Crocs, and cleaning his pool, or playing tennis at our local club, or swimming in the glorious Pacific Ocean. Occasionally I'd come home from teaching tired and troubled by work issues, at which point David would say, "Qantas time". He could not wait to get back to Australia and live permanently in our home. We acknowledged that we had the best of both worlds, knowing if the world went belly up, we could dash back to Australia and live peacefully with space and endless sunshine. Our homeward bound plan was in place.

* * *

In 2009, spring came early. April was unusually sunny with no sign of morning dew, which had evaporated by the time we got out of bed. So we decided to spend a weekend in Paris, taking the train from St Pancras, travelling light. We both enjoyed not over-planning, taking each city as we found it, lobbing into the nearest accommodation when fatigue took over. For years we'd stayed in 5-star hotels worldwide when touring with Sadler's Wells Royal Ballet, so hotel luxury was no big deal to us. This particular weekend was spent visiting galleries and rummaging through markets for the odd piece of Moorcroft. David mentioned a few times during our travels that the pain in his back, which he'd noticed a few weeks earlier, was recurring. He put it down to teaching, or simply to age.

By the time we arrived back in London the pain had increased, causing him extreme discomfort on the intake of each breath. It was unlike David to mention aches or pains. He'd always taken a casual approach to body pain and would brush off any suggestion of going to see a doctor or physiotherapist. Since I needed to attend a previously made appointment to see my doctor, David reluctantly agreed to join me, as the pain was now in his chest and getting worse. I recognised his symptoms as possibly a cracked rib, an injury dancers frequently endure. It's a painful condition and there is no treatment other than rest and time. Dr Huddy was her usual, cool self, dealing first with my issue and then considering what I had mentioned about David's chest pain. While examining David she seemed to spend considerable time probing his abdomen, after which she volunteered that she did not think he had a cracked rib. She asked if we'd be willing to go to Charing Cross Hospital the following day for David to have a precautionary scan. As it was a working week we were put out by the prospect of having to take a morning away from work for a doctor's appointment. David, in his usual dismissive way when it came to health matters, pulled a face and complained that we had created a huge fuss, and that it was far better to just get on with life.

That evening we took a stroll to Hammersmith by the river, stopping for food shopping on the way home. The morning appointment at Charing Cross Hospital was the last thing on our minds. Dr Huddy had rather casually said, "Petal, go with David for the scan", a comment that didn't seem at all odd. I remember thinking *good on Dr Huddy; she wants to make sure David shows up tomorrow.*

I knew it was important to keep the appointment, though the timing was difficult. My students were learning a ballet for their end-of-year performance to be danced at the Royal Opera House. It was a challenging work for graduate students, Frederick Ashton's *The Dream*, which I had danced when I had my run-in with Rudolf Nureyev years before. We had recently started teaching the complex choreography. I was assisting choreologist Christopher Carr from The Royal Ballet and, once the steps were taught, I would be responsible for keeping the ballet in perfect shape for the Royal Opera House performance.

Working towards the end-of-year performance is always a stressful time for students. Casting hangs in the air, as well as the search for available contracts. The top international companies will have, by then, selected the graduate-year dancers of their choice, their hiring dependent on the availability of contracts and money. Some of the students will have secured contracts after the Christmas break; others are left dangling, hoping for a last-minute offer. The atmosphere is tense. The lucky ones try not to be overly excited regarding their good fortune for fear of upsetting the less fortunate. Those still waiting for an offer plummet into desperation, and an atmosphere of urgency permeates the school. Many ballet students guard their emotions, hiding their tears; others are eager to share, and seek comfort. The teachers are aware of the tension within the graduate year, as ambition and despair frequently collide, causing angst within the group.

A steady dose of encouragement along with an understanding of their fears and disappointments needs to be at hand. I like to add an unexpected trickle of humour, along with an appreciation of their enormous effort in arriving at The Royal Ballet School's highest level.

David's workload at London Studio Centre was also accelerating with end-of-year performances. Despite all this, the next morning was like every other. David hopped out of bed, returning with freshly brewed coffee and toast. Early morning was our treasured time. We'd spend the next half hour chatting over travel plans, his Moorcroft or various work issues. We never ever deviated from our time together in bed before our day started.

We arrived at Charing Cross Hospital well before David's appointment. The scanning team were running on time, which would enable us to be back at work before lunch. Our day passed, as did dinner at home that night, during which we received a call from our GP's office asking if we could both pop into the surgery early the next morning. David's scans were back. We were shocked, having expected to wait for days if not weeks for the results. Good old National Health on the ball was our thinking. The instant results and need to see Dr Huddy straight away didn't worry us. We were certainly not expecting serious news.

Once in the surgery, Dr Huddy told us to sit down. She then said the result from the scans was not good. They had revealed cancerous tumours. More scans were needed immediately, and it was necessary to return to Charing Cross Hospital the next day. We were stunned, but consoled with the knowledge that cancer is fairly common these days, and that treatment is widely available. Also, how bad could it be? David was terrifyingly fit for a 63-year-old, with a body to put Michelangelo's David to shame. He was in peak condition, playing competition tennis in Australia, swimming

60 laps in our pool twice a day and, when in London, swimming on the weekend and teaching all day... how ill could he be?

The scan took place as soon as we arrived the next morning, after which we were told to wait; the oncologist would speak to us shortly. We went outside the hospital and sat in the April sunshine. By then, both of us were consumed with what ifs. We didn't speak. We simply held hands. And waited. Eventually, we were called back into the hospital and ushered into a small room with five screens. The oncologist introduced himself and said he would be looking after David from now on. He then indicated the images on the screens and said, "Cancer is showing on both your lungs, David, and in your bones and in your liver. It is aggressive and I'm doubtful chemotherapy will help. However, if you would like to try, I'll be willing to start you on a course of chemotherapy." Moments passed before David replied, saying he'd like time to think. He then asked, "How long have I got without chemotherapy?" "Three months," the doctor said.

That day, we met David's pain manager, a nice chap who provided us with morphine should David's pain increase. We could not have known the monumental role pain was going play in our lives during the months ahead. When we left the hospital, I remember we walked and walked around Hammersmith and Shepherd's Bush, finally arriving back in our little flat. That afternoon I called Gailene at the school and told her that, given David's dire diagnosis, I wouldn't be coming back to work for a while. Gailene, and the entire school and Royal Ballet company, would remain tirelessly supportive throughout our final months, staying in touch through Rachel Hollings – Gailene's assistant, and a dear friend of mine – who would keep everyone informed.

In the next hours we were numb and silent. The reality that David was going to die crashed around in our heads.

Rigid with fear, I fumbled about in the kitchen, trying to put some food on the table. David was in pain. He asked for his first dose of morphine. I gave it to him. We picked away at our food and then panic engulfed us. I threw myself into his arms, my silent sobbing shook us both. David did his best to stay solid, but he was flagging. He let go of me, saying he felt sick as he headed for the bathroom, but instead he collapsed and landed on the floor. I dashed to my neighbour Jenni, and together we got him downstairs into a cab and headed to Charing Cross Accident and Emergency, where the staff acted quickly. We were told David's liver was not processing the morphine he'd taken before dinner, and he needed to stay in Critical Care. By then he had turned orange. I hardly recognised my David.

* * *

The following days at Charing Cross Hospital entailed endless medication. The chemotherapy was causing intolerable sickness, prompting David to request they stop the treatment. Information poured into me, most of which I struggled to understand. I stayed at the hospital all day, dashing home to the flat at about 3am each morning to have a shower before dashing back. I could see the hospital from our apartment window, and remember thinking as dawn was breaking *for God's sake someone tell me this is not happening*. I'd had little sleep during this time, and cried a lot, which was draining my reserves. My tears were never far away. I knew when they were about to surface, and I'd escape from David to a private, safe place. But, at times, tears would pour without warning down my face. Once David asked me to please stop crying, but mostly he'd hold me until my weeping subsided. I've never forgotten the silent sobbing that would unexpectedly overtake my body, rupturing my insides.

I began to dread these gut-wrenching episodes. They were new to me and felt like physical punishment—but the sight of David struggling gave me the certainty that I would not, and could not, cave in. He was depending on me to be there, and I was determined to hold onto him for as long as I could. Curiously, after he died, the silent sobbing ceased.

* * *

Days merged into each other as I continually told myself: *do not stop, do not stop, just keep going.* The daily routine on the ward became familiar. Changes of medication, pain assessments, counsellors, a constant stream of caretaking. Life on the oncology ward is grim. There is little privacy, and the gaunt, frightened faces of the patients are a stern reminder of what lies ahead. I tried to get food into David, but mostly he had no appetite, and if he did manage to eat it came back up. Thankfully there were moments of light relief. On one occasion, while shuffling David to the shower, his hospital gown flew open down the back exposing his bottom, back and legs. Instantly, David called out to one of the staff nurses "Ahh… caught you looking at my arse." She and I fell about laughing. This was a most unlikely outburst from gentlemanly, quietly spoken David that the staff nurse, winking at me, attributed to his recent dose of morphine!

I was attending to all of David's needs other than his medication, and the staff were happy for me to do so. I was becoming more and more protective of him, longing to get him home where we could snuggle in and enjoy some privacy. During our first few days on the ward the team had agreed that, in time, I could take David home, and that was something we could look forward to.

* * *

It had been ten days since we'd arrived at Charing Cross Hospital and decisions needed to be made. The staff sister asked to see me, explaining that David could no longer remain in hospital care and that going home was no longer a realistic option due to his already challenging pain. To keep David comfortable, she said, the medication required could only be administered by a professional. She then gently suggested I go immediately to Pembridge Hospice near Ladbroke Grove. David needed rest and palliative care as soon as possible. My brain shattered. I was exploding. My hurt was so immense that I wanted to run and keep running. How was I going to tell David he was never going home again? I could not utter those words for fear of making them a reality. I ran out of the hospital straight into cold air. I was not dressed for being outside, and the day was cold and grey. I couldn't stop. I had to keep going. I knew what I had to do. I grabbed a cab and arrived at Pembridge Hospice, breathless and frozen. I'd walked this path before with Michael and all I could think was *this is fucking unfair.* I introduced myself at the desk to a kindly nurse, who gently talked me through the procedure of admitting a patient. The atmosphere was gentle, homely and terrifyingly quiet. When I left the hospice, I needed to walk before facing David. No matter how strong I looked to others I was unravelling. Hope had faded, and no amount of strength and will was going to change our future.

I arrived back on the ward longing to see David. Then it was time to summon the strength to tell him what needed to happen now. David, always mindful of taking care of me, asked no questions. He knew the answers, and sought to protect me from further inquiry. This was one of the many things I loved so much about him. He never pushed a point and knew when to pull back. But the cruel realisation that we would never again live in our home pierced into us. With eyes smarting we held onto each other, feeling ambushed and powerless. There was no place to hide. Cancer had taken possession of us by force. David was flushing, his beautiful eyes pleading and sad. I could not look at him as I foraged to find plastic bags, shovelling into them the bits gathered during our two-week stay in Charing Cross Hospital. Pretending to busy myself helped me to stuff down the screams rupturing my throat.

There we were, packed and ready to move to Pembridge Hospice. We may have looked like an organised couple, though nothing could have been further from the truth. Our life was in chaos. It would never be the same again.

* * *

At the hospice we were taken to David's room, which was a beaming shade of yellow. It was a good size and overlooked a tiny courtyard shaded from sunlight, which no doubt prompted the yellow décor. When stuck in the very worst life can offer, small comforts, like a yellow room, are seen as gifts from nowhere. I settled us both into what was to become our home for the time we had left. The staff visited frequently that day: there were examinations, food requirements, the pain team—an endless stream of kind people going about their work as they attended to David. Throughout this time, he was passive. I could see him processing every move his team made as they saw to his care. He hated the attention. His constant reminders to the nurses to feed me as well as him sparked a glimmer of hope that my darling, caring David was still with us.

I listened carefully to every nurse and doctor, taking notes as reminders in case I missed anything important regarding David's care. The team realised I was not leaving and offered to bring in a bed for me. We were safe, tucked into our small, comfortable room. I felt a sense of relief knowing help was at hand for David at any given moment.

I knew I could rely on my adrenaline which, in this state of crisis, would allow me to forge ahead and get us settled. It was reminiscent of my childhood, preparing my mother's bag as she left for weeks on end to have hospital treatment, all the while hiding my tears knowing she'd be gone for a long time and hating the thought of being without her. And it recalled packing up and sorting Michael for his stay at Mildmay Mission Hospice. So I knew what to do. I had trodden the stepping stones.

We were two weeks into our three-month life span. David, at this stage, was walking, albeit gingerly due to rapid weight loss. Weather permitting, we'd spend time outside in the garden and, just for a moment, we'd manage to forget that our days together were ending. A concoction of medication was keeping David's discomfort at bay. Top-ups came on a regular basis, allowing time and energy for respite and recharging. I was comforted by the knowledge that, being in hospice care, David's end of life would be as Michael's had been: spared of anguish and pain when his time came to die. Though, as I would learn, the truth was otherwise.

* * *

From the start of his diagnosis, David did not want to see or speak to anyone. On a few occasions I asked if he was willing to talk to his family. His reply was always the same: this is our time, it is all we have, and I have no energy to spread myself further. I could not question David's decision. He was never one for negotiation once he'd made up his mind. I had to stop asking, and I did, but I knew that once David died I would have to explain his choice to his family, and this weighed heavily on me.

In fact, David's family was small. His mother, Joan, had left their home when David was a very young boy. He was brought up by his father and his stepmother Edith, a well-read, thoughtful woman. Shortly before David became ill, he decided to find his birth mother. Their reunion was good. To my knowledge David had never been given a reason why she left the family home. He held no outward grudge towards her, but it had been important to him that he find her. They managed to meet up on one other occasion before Joan died. David left much unsaid, which I had always wondered about. Only rarely would he talk to me about why no one had given him an explanation about his mother's absence.

At an early age, encouraged by Edith, David developed a love of music, which in due course led him to ballet. Not only did he immediately enjoy ballet, it was soon recognised that he had potential. His ballet classes became his safe world, leading him into an unimaginable life of devotion, and a passion of which he would never be free. So often we'd agree about how lucky we were to have found work we loved and were rather good at.

* * *

In those early days at the hospice, my strength remained intact in spite of no family support system at hand. I called Australia on a regular basis to speak with my niece and sister. They were always generous and kind. Knowing I would always have their love and care was a vital source of nourishment. Also in Australia was my dear friend Marilyn Rowe, the only person I knew who'd experienced the same trauma and loss. In my darkest hours I would take strength from knowing that she had lived through this nightmare and survived. But lurking inside my head, as I imagined what lay ahead, I found myself asking, *Why David? Why?* And then I wondered if I would be able to remain solid for him throughout this infernal punishment.

The days passed. Soon, we completed one of the three months David had left. One afternoon, he wanted to go back to our flat in Shepherd's Bush. We packed a bag of medication, called a cab, and off we went. As soon as we arrived at the flat David said he wanted to work on a list of things that would help me get our house in Australia up and running without him. He knew I had no idea of these functions and would be at a total loss. I needed to know how to reset the heating boiler, where the stopcocks were, what the codes were for the alarm system and swimming pool regulator, phone numbers for our gardener, pool maintenance chap, car mechanic and so on. I hid my tears as we worked through his instructions. I was in adoration of his care for me, his strength and meticulous way of handing over to me the fundamentals of our life. Yet, as I wrote down what he told me, I was screaming inside.

When we finished, he asked to go out onto the patio overlooking London, where he stood for some time. His beautiful upright back was now painfully thin, hunched and frail as he stood there, remembering summer nights on that patio when we sat with glasses of Merlot and watched the London sunset. After a while he called me over, put his arms around me and said, "Hold onto me won't you Nutty."

I held on.

Moments later he said, "Let's go darling." As we were leaving the building, I knew he was saying goodbye, in the understanding that he'd never return to our home.

I kept telling myself this was not the end of our life. We still had time. And, for now, I had to get David safely back to the hospice.

* * *

During the following few weeks, our daily life was eaten up with repeated visits from the palliative nurses and various people checking something or other. I was caring for David's showering and eating, though food had lost its appeal due to his difficulty controlling his tongue. The nurses became part of our life, always at hand but knowing when to be invisible and never misjudging David's need for relief from pain which, at this stage, was relatively under control. There were times when my skin would crawl, and I'd want to look away from David to shield myself from the truth in front of me. As I write, I'm reliving those physical attacks on my body; the sensations that traumatised me for years after David died.

In the afternoon, on a few occasions, we still managed to sit outside in the hospice garden for a short time until David felt cold. Night-time brought him temporary respite and, after he fell asleep, I'd walk the dimly lit corridors of the hospice, ending up in the sitting area reserved for relatives, where tea and coffee were always at hand. Lone figures, relatives with sad eyes, would drift by exchanging knowing looks with me. As the weeks passed, one by one they would no longer be there; a reminder that in time I too would be gone.

Members of the staff frequently sat beside me. We had nothing to say but their presence close by was comforting. David would often wake during the night needing the bathroom. I'd be awake and off the bed before he moved. I hated going to sleep – I begrudged any time away from David – and I was functioning in a perpetual state of alertness; something I'd not experienced before. I was constantly busy, wiping down his body, trying to keep him cool, cleaning his mouth, coaxing tiny sips of water, massaging his feet, changing his pillows to find a more comfortable position. Anything to bring some small relief.

On those occasions, terror pushed me forward. I was always running, grabbing cabs, jumping on buses, anything to get me back to David in fear that he might die while I was away. And at times, when panic overtook me, I'd go and sit in a church. Just being around like-minded, quiet people soothed me, and I would return to David feeling steadier and refreshed.

I also found comfort at a special place in West London called Maggie's, a cancer support centre, which sheltered me as, day by day, my world fell apart. There is no reception desk at Maggie's, and no questions asked. What you encounter is the scent of coffee, a table with newspapers, biscuits and many books encased in a building created by England's most prominent architects Richard Rogers and Ivan Harbour. Drenched in light and warmth, Maggie's provides free support for families and people living with cancer. Counsellors stroll by with welcoming arms, ready to listen, gently stroke or advise.

There are 24 Maggie's centres across the UK, each individual in appearance. Renowned architects queue to design these centres; among them, Frank Gehry and Zaha Hadid. Their style is important – for it is reported that "architectural environments can significantly affect a patient's recovery time" – and each centre is built at the invitation of the NHS trust, usually in the surrounds of hospitals and oncology centres. Maggie's was founded by a remarkable woman, Maggie Keswick Jencks who, when living with advanced cancer, devoted her short life to creating a place of beauty where those dealing with life-threatening cancer can feel safe and warm. For me, the lovely, nourishing centre was a haven.

* * *

Being in reasonably calm waters allowed us time to talk. David never once mentioned dying, but it troubled him that we had not had children. I remember him saying "How much better it would be for you, darling, if our baby had survived. You are going to need comforting. Tell me that you will accept all the help offered to you and make no major decisions for two years."

I reassured him saying, "David, I will remember and act on every word you've ever said to me."

He stared into my eyes.

"Promise," he said, as I reached for his hand. And I promised.

One day, out of nowhere, he looked at me through sunken eyes and said, "Our ballet family will be there for you." This I already knew to be true, and I could see how much comfort it gave him.

***

By the end of our second month David was experiencing more pain in different parts of his body. The cancer was creeping all over him. Weight loss and lying in bed put pressure on his joints, causing bed sores to erupt on the base of his spine. The nurses hardly left our side as recurring waves of torment became more and more frequent. Their kindness and gentleness were precious gifts as we entered the final weeks of our life together.

David was experiencing what is known as breakthrough pain, which lurked day and night, crashing in on him without warning. It was intolerable, beating his body relentlessly. His agonised cries were to haunt me for a long time. I'd run to the nurse's station alerting the staff, who would administer Fentanyl, a drug that would stop his thrashing pain momentarily. He took beating after beating as the pain team struggled to help him, mostly without success.

I now know that lung, bone and liver cancers are the hardest to control. I believe that, had we known this when he was diagnosed, we'd have considered going to the Dignitas Clinic in Switzerland, where the suffering can choose to "die with dignity". But, having experienced Michael's death, I had been convinced that extreme pain can be arrested as Michael's was when dying of AIDS. David's suffering would teach me that this is not always the case.

A few days before David died came the pink wedge of sponge on a short stick. It's used to moisten the mouth and provide a small amount of liquid to a dying person. This was not new to me. I'd done this for Michael and witnessed the pleasure that tiny amount of moisture could bring. David's beautiful lips were cracked and dry. As I put the pink sponge near his mouth, his blue eyes would half open and his lips would part like a tiny bird begging for food from its mother. I had not touched or held David since we were at our flat, on the patio. Weeks had passed since then. He'd been in too much distress and pain to tolerate physical contact other than from the nurses who needed to attend to him.

During the last days of David's life, I begged his palliative doctor to give him more help. She did only what she felt she was allowed to do. It was not enough. I felt David's suffering could have been curbed; he'd been left to suffer way too long. When it was suggested, and not for the first time, that chemotherapy be added to David's medication at this late stage as it could lessen his pain, his palliative care doctor replied, "Frankly I wouldn't bother." I was incensed, certain that caring for the dying had left her desensitised. I will never ever forget the silence between us that followed that thoughtless reply. She may as well have said... "you're finished David. No point." Had she forgotten how valuable the final weeks and days of her patients' lives are to them?

David's last days were wracked with endless brutal beatings that flogged his body relentlessly as he screamed for help which, when it came, brought little relief. In spite of my pleas to his pain team, his suffering continued, and they allowed it. I held onto his hands, reminding him that he was not alone. And I prayed that he would find peace. I was astounded by the strength in his wafer-thin body, which enabled him to thrash about in response to the fierce waves of pain. He was desperately wounded and at the mercy of his team, who seemed to have done all they could, or would, do. Finally, I crawled onto the bed and held onto his beautiful face to stop him violently bashing his head from side to side. My holding his face seemed to bring about a calmness. His strength was fading. The pain had gotten its way. I kept whispering to him, making sure he knew I was there. Then, for the first time ever, I watched my beautiful David physically weaken. His breath quietened and he opened his eyes. For one second I thought he was going to speak to me, but he simply inhaled one more silent breath and stopped moving, his eyes wide and frozen, as if he was looking at me. I knew at that moment his cancer had won. It had beaten him to death and changed our lives forever.

At last, David was free of pain. I climbed into bed with him, holding him, no longer fearing I might hurt or bruise his frail, beautiful body. At last, I had a soft place to fall, even if only for a brief time. Just us, curled up together, as we had so often been. I closed my eyes. The staff left us alone for a while. Then, together, we washed David, allowing me to gaze one last time at his beautifully shaped ballet legs and feet, which I'd always adored. Then, very gently, I covered him.

My comfort came from knowing my beautiful husband would never be far from my thoughts and would continue to love and comfort me as he had done for the greater part of my adult life.

* * *

The day after David's death, I asked for a meeting with the hospice team. I wanted to thank them for their care during our ten-week stay, but also to explain how disappointed I was that David had been allowed to suffer so much for so long. Their response was that, on reflection, perhaps his medication during the last days had been too conservative. Indeed. It was.

After that meeting, one of the nurses stopped me as I was leaving. She said, "David's death was the worst I've experienced, so disturbing that a member of our team has been badly shaken." I put my arms around her and, for a moment, we were bound together in recognition of the fact that she had lived his death with me.

After that, all I remember is arriving at our flat, lying on the floor and hearing myself howl. I was broken, torn apart, not knowing how I could go on living without David. There was a loud knocking on my door and there stood my kind neighbour, Jenni Sivertsen, in her dressing gown, holding milk and tea bags. She came in, put the kettle on, and held onto me curled up on the floor. I don't remember for how long. I will never forget the warmth and strength she mustered for me. She had known our situation from the night we left for Charing Cross. It was Jenni I'd gone to for help in getting David downstairs and into a cab. My cries that morning told her that he had died, and I was back at the flat alone.

* * *

Arranging David's funeral became my main occupation. It was the last and only thing I could do for him. Despite my wishful thinking that none of this was happening, I managed to assemble a funeral plan. My sister arrived from Perth, which was a blessing for me. Knowing how David hated to be the centre of attention unless he was on stage, the funeral was to be family only, followed eventually by the memorial service, a gathering for friends, which I would plan and hold later in the summer. My mind was fragmented, unsettled with misleading and erratic thoughts of where I would go and what I would do. All I wanted was to be with David.

The funeral manager was a kind woman who, seeing my desperation and sadness, agreed that I could visit David every day during the week before his funeral. This was precious time for me. I needed to be sure David really was never going to look at me again. For days I went to be beside him, my sister waiting in the reception area. She remained gentle and kind to me, never questioning my need to sit with David's body. He had never spoken about his dying, though I did recall a conversation we'd had years before, during which we'd both said we would want to be cremated. Knowing how David would have hated the commotion of a public funeral, and mindful of his family's shock and pain, I decided on a private funeral. That would be best for me as well, as I was threadbare, and barely standing. I knew that friends, students and fans would want to celebrate David and his career, but a memorial service would have to wait until strength and peace returned. Assuming they ever did.

As I recall, just seven of us gathered. The service was simple, and the only music played was "Woman", a song John Lennon wrote for Yoko Ono. David loved that song, and on Saturday nights, at our home in Australia, he devised what he called our "party night", which was always accompanied by a top drop of cooling white wine. We'd play our favourite songs, "Woman" in particular, which was on the CD of Lennon's final album that David had bought for me. Off we'd swing, dancing around our billiard room. Then we'd jump into our flood-lit swimming pool, just the two of us, mad about each other, frolicking until the small hours.

When the service ended, I collected David's ashes. I carried them around with me everywhere for days—a private need that brought me comfort. His ashes remain with me to this day. He once told me that he would like them to come to rest in his beloved Australia, and when I make my final journey back home that is where they will be.

* * *

For some time after David's death the place I most wanted to be was in a Catholic church, surrounded by like-minded people. Having been convent educated by the Sisters of Mercy, and having a mother who was a staunch Catholic, I had followed suit.

A few weeks after the funeral, I began planning David's memorial, which I had scheduled for late August. Anything I could do related to David gave me pleasure and a sense of purpose and energy. It was almost as if he'd never left. As the days passed, I began to think that a break away from London would help clear my head. I decided to go to Melbourne. The responsibility of our empty home there hung over me. Still, paramount in my mind was that David had told me not to make any major decisions for two years. I knew my current state of mind was unreliable, so I followed his admonition precisely. Four years would pass before I made the decision to sell our beloved home.

* * *

As soon as I returned to Australia I knew I'd set myself too big a task. It broke me to enter our home with no David beside me, knowing there would never be David beside me ever again. I was nowhere near ready to consider my future. Stepping off the plane in Melbourne I fell into the arms of my dear friend Lisa Pavane who, along with her husband Robert Marshall, took me to their cosy home for the following few weeks. My Australian Ballet family soon gathered, just as

David had said they would. I will never forget their love and kindness.

It was during this time that my morning horrors began. Every morning, on waking, my first thought would be *thank God it was only a dream; I'll open my eyes and the nightmare will have gone*. I dreaded coming out of sleep to be greeted by the horrible truth that David had died and wasn't coming back. Rage would erupt inside of me. One thought was to plague me for years to come: why did the palliative team let him suffer so much for so long? Finally, I'd fall out of bed, exhausted. My morning horrors were never far away. Going to sleep I could find no peace. Physical shudders overtook my body as I relived David's cries for help when his pain became intolerable. Then there were the lifelike dreams in which I would see him right there before me. These were the dreams I longed for, dreams that made the heartbreaking disappointment when I awakened worthwhile. Just to have seen him one more time.

During the following two weeks it was comforting to talk about David to our friends, who wanted to hear how his life had ended, and were keen to celebrate his goodness. Their love and respect for him were overwhelming and made it easy for me to share in their grief. Going to Australia had given me time to process what had happened. The plane ride back to London gave me an opportunity to begin mentally preparing myself for life there without David. I've always used planes as a private thinking space, free from interruptions. Wandering to my seat, I adopted my freeze body language just in case a potential gabber was already seated next to me. Usually, my do-not-disturb signals were blatant enough to ward off any talking.

At home, I had much to do as I finalised David's memorial arrangements and prematurely thought about going back to work. London was busy, sunny and warm.

I switched to autopilot and was grateful for the warmth and reassurance our flat offered. That tiny space overlooking West London on the eighth floor was never intended to be a permanent living space; it was our bolt hole, a resting place convenient for work commitments.

To my relief, being back in London made me feel safe and secure. My ballet family were never far away and wanting to know about David's memorial, and to talk about him. Their care and attention were a source of comfort. Even so, my mind was often all over the place and I longed for David, especially during the early hours of the morning, when I'd find myself sitting by the window looking down to Shepherd's Bush Road, sharing London with maybe one lone figure. I felt passive, with no need to appear anything other than whatever I was at that moment.

* * *

Summer that year was as glorious as an English summer can possibly be. The day of David's memorial was especially warm, bright and sunny. My dear friend Margaret Mercer flew from Perth to be by my side, and my niece Carina arrived from Australia, generous and loving as always. Her presence signalled that I had family support, albeit in small number.

The church in Covent Garden was packed to capacity. Seeing so many people I'd never expected filled me with a warmth I will never forget. I felt strengthened by their outpouring of affection for me and their love for David. Carina's eulogy was heartfelt as she shared the important role Uncle David had played in her children's upbringing when he was the only man in their lives they could trust and depend on. He had played games with them, and swam way out into Sydney's sea with Lydia on his back. Her brother

Michael had joined him in looking at trucks and all things mechanical.

During other eulogies, unforgettable words of respect and inspiration were spoken about David—all of them true. David Bintley, Director of Sadler's Wells Royal Ballet, remembered the opening night of Peter Wright's new production of *Swan Lake,* which featured David as Prince Siegfried. It had been massively expensive; we all knew the critical importance of its success. So much rested on the performances of the leading dancers and, as David Bintley remembered, "David Ashmole was the man for the job."

After words of love had been spoken, one of our Royal Ballet School pianists, Dr Alastair Bannerman, generously agreed to play the pas de deux from Frederick Ashton's ballet *The Dream*, in which the role of Oberon had been dear to David's heart. Bannerman also played Prince Siegfried's solo from Act I of *Swan Lake*; another ballet and role David was well known for and had loved dearly. This beautiful music evoked treasured memories for everyone present on that sunny London day, bringing to mind indelible images of David doing what he loved most of all.

* * *

David's death had torn me away from my work, my creative life. Part of me thought that getting back into my safe space of teaching would allow me to come up for air. But instinct told me otherwise. I was in no way ready to face my students, despite missing them terribly. Watching my dancers' development had always provided nourishment for me, and in return I would share with them everything I knew. I would smile on overhearing dancers refer to me as their ballet geek! I loved every aspect of teaching: keeping an eye on the late bloomer, reining in the galloping horse and relentlessly reinforcing technical information. My dancers knew I was a stickler for detail; at the same time they appreciated my quirky sense of humour. Frequently – after an impossibly challenging day, taking another tip from Professor Comte – laughter was always the best way to end a demanding workload. I needed to get back into the studio with them. But it was too soon.

* * *

That summer was long and warm. It passed almost without my noticing. David's death had traumatised me. I could not express myself, nor rid myself from wanting him back. Like the mother elephant in mourning supported by her aunties, my sisterhood clocked in to grieve with me in every which way they could. Each time I thrashed around, someone from my ballet family would somehow appear or call. My sister and niece were constantly making contact from Australia to see how I was. With no immediate family on hand the fact that my friends stayed in touch helped me deal with my loss. I don't remember thinking I was depressed, and I don't remember feeling bad; I simply did not feel. I stopped travelling on the tube because for some reason I'd face the door between carriages and cry. I'm not sure why this would happen, but it did. Perhaps seeing others buttoned up and going about their day heightened my sense of lack of purpose.

I remember refusing to lie down or let go even when I was kaput, finished. The prospect of eventually going back to work was my motivation to heal. Throughout my life, it was my work that had kept me upright, giving me strength when things started to unravel. Work was the stabilising thing I could count on. It fuelled my confidence, ignited my passion and I was good at it. Like the students I taught, from an early age I had had a plan. In my case, nothing was going to stop me from seeking the physical sensation I first experienced back in my dancing school with Madam. These days this sensation has a name; it's called "flow". This particular sensation eludes many dancers, keeping them one small step away from true artistry. Flow can be encouraged and explored with the help of a knowledgeable coach; however, a natural sense of flow is bestowed upon a very few. It is described as "a state of complete immersion in an activity". A state of flow is not exclusive; anyone can experience it. As a teacher/choreographer and certainly as a dancer it was my most intoxicating perception, and explains my own addiction to dance that has never left.

Still, I could not return to the world of dance. At least not yet.

* * *

By the end of the following year, I'd experienced a rollercoaster of feelings—some heartbreaking, others comforting. I'd had time to reflect on our 30-year marriage. I loved remembering our intimate life and times of fun and laughter. I'd had more than a year away from work, and knew that if I could get back into the studio I'd regain my emotional strength. Instead, I spiralled into a constant longing for David, which would not let up. I decided that if I could see no way of living without David my only option was to die. I fashioned a meticulous plan that served as my fail-safe option: eight steps from the tube tunnel wall to the edge of the platform and then onto the tracks was all it would take to end my wanting him. Knowing there was a way out, I no longer felt pressurised into making the most of what felt like a horrible life.

Yet I pressed on, as well I could, because I had to. Finally – more than a year after David died – I decided it was time to

157

return to teaching. I found myself longing for my students. I was well aware that I'd suddenly abandoned them; how must that have felt for them during their graduation final year? It also occurred to me that I needed to appreciate and acknowledge the abundance of love and care bestowed on me by my friends at The Royal Ballet School during my darkest days. To do that, I told myself, I must get back into the studio, be in flow with my dancers, teach them and gaze again at their work. I yearned to hear my pianist Elvira Gavrilova play my favourite adage music, the piece she'd kept especially for me at my request.

* * *

Once back with the dancers I felt re-energised. The Royal Ballet School welcomed me with warmth and kindness, expressing joy at having Miss Miller, as I was known there, back on board. The talented third-year graduate students I had left the previous year were all high-flyers, getting on with their contracts worldwide. My new third-year graduates were equally inspiring and welcoming. I couldn't wait to get them working to their maximum potential, knowing that by the end of the year it would be their turn to secure contracts and fly away.

It would be impossible for me not to consider my time at The Royal Ballet School as The Golden Years. My students included Vadim Muntagirov: quiet, reserved, and speaking no English, who arrived at the school from Russia. Initially, he stayed well back in the class until his natural talent exploded. Other students for whom I had what proved to be justifiably high hopes were Yasmine Naghdi, Shiori Kase, Francesca Hayward, Dylan Gutierrez, Jonathan Hanks, Hannah Rudd, Bethany Kingsley-Garner, Claire Calvert, Benjamin Ella, Millis Faust, Adeline Kaiser, Sergei Polunin,

Liam Scarlett, Reece Clarke, Brandon Lawrence, William Bracewell, Matthew Ball, Grete Sofie Borud Nybakken, Roseanna Leney, Bruno Micchiardi, Douwe Dekkers, Dario Elia, Jacopo Belussi, Lucas Lima and Charlie Peters. They were all eager high-flyers, passionate Top Guns. These young, fledgling dancers, and many others, unknowingly taught me more than I could have ever imagined. I was the lucky teacher to have those sparks of talent on my watch.

Being a teacher of the graduate class at The Royal Ballet School came with high expectations. In anticipation of their offer of contracts with major ballet companies, I needed to accelerate them to a professional level, both technically and mentally. The responsibility of having in my care the most talented young dancers in the world was something I took to heart. I was accountable for their progress in every way. I knew they were counting on my corrections and advice. Yet I was often bewildered by the way in which their hunger to learn and their fearlessness was offset by their vulnerability. In the past, I'd often turned to David, seeking his sage advice on how much correction to give and when to give it.

Days, weeks and months passed. I still longed for David, but I was coping. I'd made a start.

***

After two years back at The Royal Ballet School, I found myself longing to visit our beloved Greek Island, Hydra. Thoughts of the island evoked vivid memories of David and me relishing sun-filled summers languishing there. It had been our hideaway, our precious place to recover and treat our bodies to a well-earned rest. Every day, David would make the long swim from Kamini beach to Cafe Spelia perched on the rocks, where I'd be waiting, slightly terrified that he'd be mowed down en route by one of the boat taxies. I need not have worried. David was a strong swimmer, and his innate fearlessness protected him from negative thoughts of potential danger. Often, I'd swim out to meet him, and we'd frolic in the warm Adriatic Sea, finally arriving back at Spelia for a Greek salad and local wine before retreating to bed for a love-filled afternoon. In the cool of our room we'd hide away from the heat of the day, emerging around eight o'clock for another evening swim, checking out numerous galleries on our way up to Anita's Taverna for a slap-up Greek dinner.

My longing for Hydra did not subside, so the following summer I took off for Athens, then caught the bus to Piraeus and then boarded the hydrofoil, which pounded its way through the Aegean Sea. I knew the route very well, but this was the first time in many years I'd travelled there alone... no David.

From my first visit to Hydra, the island and its people captured my heart. I had been married to Michael then, and on my own, as I danced with Sadler's Wells Royal Ballet in Athens at the Herod Atticus arena, in performances led by Dame Margot Fonteyn. By chance, my dancing partner Graeme Powell introduced me to his friend Lilly Mac who lived on Hydra. I was smitten by this enigmatic, wild, irresistible Russian who reminded me of Madam Kira Bousloff, my first ballet teacher. Lilly invited me to the island that summer. I was aroused and intrigued by the artists who had gravitated to this tiny jewel of a place. And so began my lifelong love affair with Hydra, Lilly, her children and grandchildren, to whom I refer to affectionately as my Russian/Greek family.

My early visits to the island used to occupy my entire August summer break from Sadler's Wells Royal Ballet. Blue tables, blue chairs, blue doors and the bluest of blue skies stood out among the little white houses and pink bougainvillea, which cascaded everywhere. My accommodation was humble; I slept wherever I could find a cheap bed as I had few funds, so whatever I could find had to be basic. Things always fell my way somehow. Lilly frequently came up with someone's spare balcony space, an empty room or a vacant studio.

Lilly also gathered me into her flock of writers, poets, painters—all speaking different languages at the same time, no one taking a breath but somehow each seeming to understand the others. Leonard Cohen and his love Marianne were there intermittently, along with other known artists, but to me they were simply people spending time on the island. I was curious, surrounded by this colourful, intense group that filtered in and out of Lilly's house. There were copious amounts of delicious food. Retsina and Ouzo accompanied feisty, fascinating conversations that extended late into the night. I was not fazed, but wondered what on earth I could possibly contribute to this group of wild, artistic intellectuals. I was naïve, curious and utterly intoxicated by my surroundings and this enthralling community of artistes who gravitated to this tiny island every summer. Lilly saw to it that the waif-like ballet dancer was always included in the impromptu gatherings at her house, which hung precariously on the side of a hill overlooking the sea. She was forthcoming with warnings of too much sun, sea, alcohol and late-night dancing which, on a few occasions, caught me out, rendering me horribly ill. I felt reckless, dashing forward as fast as I could, my newfound love felt easy yet wonderfully treacherous.

As the summers passed, I became one of the locals and each year learned more about Lilly and her kindness, her spirit and her occasional scary abruptness. I once asked her why she had no radio or music in her house; her disbelieving look unnerved me. I was frozen to the spot, wondering what on earth I'd said to warrant such a penetrating stare. Then the tirade commenced, with Lilly ranting at me: music, music, you ask for music, you hear nothing. Music is everywhere. The sound of the sea below, the wind thrashing into the side of the house, the distant bells on the donkeys nearby, the roosters and the shuffling of the old men scrambling up the hill. You... Petal the ballet dancer, and you hear nothing. I stood my ground. I would not allow Lilly to beat me up or leave me feeling as foolish and gauche as I did. Once her tirade had subsided, I walked away to the sound of Lilly ranting to herself in what sounded like Russian with a lot of stops and huffing and puffing.

Gradually, over the years, my financial situation improved, allowing me to upgrade my accommodation. In 2008 I decided to make the beautiful Bratsera Hotel my holiday retreat. From then on, I was welcomed as family by Janice Connock Millou and the rest of the Bratsera staff each year. My arrival at the hotel after David's death was especially memorable; the staff were kinder than ever.

Lilly died in 2008. I have remained close to her children, grandchildren and great grandchildren. One hot Hydra night, Natasha Heidsieck, Lilly's daughter, would provide the incentive I needed to explore another chapter in my life... a chapter beyond David, which at the time seemed unthinkable.

* * *

When summer ended, being back in the studio propelled me forward. My work in no way took away my longing to touch and smell David, but it tapped into an inner strength. Somehow, with the support of friends, I managed to get out of bed each day. I hated the weekends, feeling at a loss without my daily teaching programme, so I volunteered to teach the Saturday morning ballet class, which helped.

Throughout this time, I was in contact with my Australian friend Marilyn Rowe who had also lost two husbands; only she could truly speak words of compassion to me. The fact that she had survived similar loss helped me persevere. She never burdened me with advice. Her quiet, knowing tone was all I needed. In any case, there were no suitable words, no advice, no remedies or quick fixes. This trauma had a pathway of its own. I needed to sit it out and grab every bit of help and encouragement that came my way.

* * *

Gradually, during the following five years, I emerged out of the dark. Hearing my own laughter was a distinct moment of clarity; it felt okay to laugh and forget being sad. I was retrieving my power from the grief that had consumed me since David's diagnosis, and I was enjoying feeling brave. This was a slightly weird realisation, which I pondered quite a lot. The Royal Ballet School was the perfect cushion I needed as I moved from one phase of my life into another.

I continued to return to Hydra every summer and, as the years passed, the locals seemed to forget "David and Petal" and it became simply "Petal". I didn't mind. I no longer needed to share my hurt with acquaintances, as kind and well-meaning as they were. It's also true that my Russian/Greek family never forgot David and frequently, after dinner, the conversation would ramble into memories of us together. I loved that they wanted to remember us. It meant a lot to me, and I think they felt that. It was curious: on one hand I didn't want to over-talk David, but equally I didn't want him to be forgotten.

* * *

My life took on a predictable pattern: when summers ended, I returned to The Royal Ballet School. Each new term brought with it the opportunity for me to continue improving my life.

I never ceased to feel fortunate to have work I was addicted to and loved. During my ten years there I donated three of my existing pas de deux to the school, and Gailene commissioned me to choreograph four new ballets specifically designed to showcase the exceptional talent we had at the time. The students thrived on the experience of working with a choreographer and grabbing this opportunity to explore their technique. Gailene was forever pushing the school forward, and she revelled in seeing what I brought out of the students. Their talent was indeed outstanding, and making ballets for them was a responsibility I cherished. Gailene, always keen to present our high standard to the world, arranged tours of Portugal, Florida, Dresden, China—allowing the students the experience of performing these works that had been choreographed on them. Many rehearsals were conducted out of school hours and frequently I'd find myself demanding that the dancers stop practising and go home. Those fierce young sponges were a teacher's dream. I adored them.

Another thing I loved was accompanying our top graduate students to ballet competitions worldwide: Switzerland, Portugal, China, Germany, America all in the mix. I prepared my dancers with great care. Each dancer would work with me in selecting a solo most suited to their ability. This exercise was important, allowing the students an opportunity to shoulder some of the responsibility. It is common for a young dancer to choose a solo which may push them out of their depth. When this occurred we'd work through the obstacles together. If their choice proved too difficult, I would point out the importance of selecting a doable solo so that the dancer would be seen at his or her very best. Generally, they took my advice and settled for a solo appropriate for their level and ability.

* * *

The Royal Ballet School was, and is, the womb of The Royal Ballet. It is where a dancer's growth begins. After teaching at the school for ten years I knew it was time for a change. Being there had been a precious time in my life. At the end, as at the beginning, I cherished the fact that I'd been trusted to nurture, care for and develop our most talented and vulnerable young dancers.

I had been 50 years old when Gailene Stock employed me to teach there. By that time, I'd taught at schools and companies for years, and thought of myself as a knowledgeable teacher. How wrong I was. Learning the Royal Ballet School system of training had been demanding, but a challenge I had immediately loved. During my early days there I had wanted to fix everything immediately for my dancers. How tiring I must have been... I had much to learn.

Part of my duty of care had been to attend to the pastoral care of my students. Having lived with partners who were privately educated in mainstream boarding school situations I now ponder on how suitable such an environment is for young people. At White Lodge, The Royal Ballet School's boarding section, the students live in an environment of discipline. They learn to manage without parental care and deal with an institutional ballet lifestyle in preparation for that of a professional ballet dancer. They learn to fit in, participate and to accept cutting-edge competition, taking pride in going forward and achieving. It is seldom a student is found to be unhappy—they know they've been given an opportunity, and are privileged to be chosen to attend a ballet school of excellence. I fondly remember tears shed by parents and students as the youngsters were delivered to the school on that very first day. Come the arrival of return to school after first term holidays teachers are greeted by an avalanche of students running through the front door dying to hear the music and dance.

Year after year, I saw my students bloom and grow and, looking back on my time at The Royal Ballet School, I can say it was when giving to my students became a gift to me. In leaving, I was taking with me wonderful memories and friendships; some of my students would remain in my life long after my teaching days had finished. One special note from a student came from Hannah Rudd who, after a determined battle, became one of Rambert's most loved and respected dancers. Her message read, "Thank you Miss Miller for never giving up on me." I treasure her words. And, although I wasn't sure exactly what I wanted to do, my need to move on was great. And so I walked away.

* * *

I was looking forward to having space in my life and exploring new ideas—but my idea of waking up each day with no plan, facing a totally free day didn't last long. Marilyn Rowe asked if I would consider returning home and taking a teaching position at The Australian Ballet School. I was excited by the thought; at the same time was I ready for another challenge that would take me away from my London ballet family and present a new set of hills to climb?

Before I answered Marilyn, memories of my life in Australia flooded in. I thought about the punishing summers in Perth, when temperatures reach 40 degrees for days on end, parching public gardens, lawns and parks, all of them covered with leaves that fall from towering gumtrees bravely attempting to stand up to the scorching heat of the sun. I recalled the clicker clack of reticulation sprinklers that water the beautifully plucked and preened gardens of the better off as their green lawns, rose beds and hydrangeas flourish despite the torturous heat. And then there were the birds. In Australia, birds – like the landscape – are immense, and they are vocal and will not be ignored. Large sulphur-crested white cockatoos, rose pink and grey galahs, fat black and white magpies, crows, multi-coloured parakeets all unashamedly make their presence felt. The beautiful galah gets its name from the Yuwaalaraay Aboriginal people. Over generations the word "galah" has been adapted by the Australian language to describe a fool or silly person. These striking birds can be found all over Australia living in large colonies; often hundreds of them take over an entire tree. Their fun character, naughtiness and quick learning ability make them wonderful pets who can be taught to mimic words and dance. The most outspoken of all is the kookaburra, which belongs to the kingfisher family and is a chunky, strong bird capable of swooping down and stealing a sausage off the barbie or picking up a snake and dropping it to its death. Kookaburras are often human friendly; it is not uncommon for a pair to sit on a veranda waiting for a titbit of meat provided by a smitten human. Their laugh is extraordinary: loud, happy and hilarious. I remember as a child hoping the laughter was at me! Wherever one goes in Australia, birdsong follows. London and Scotland have tweeting, chirpy little birds who for me lack the character and presence of Australian birds.

As a native, I knew Australia as a diverse land that is not for the faint hearted. In addition to the punishing heat there are killer spiders, snakes, sea creatures, floods and high-speed fires that consume anything in their path: animals, people, homes, townships. These monsters cover areas as big as small counties and blaze on for weeks out of control. Something else I mused on was the Australian character. As a rule, they're an outspoken, confident people known for their quick wit and the Australian slang that peppers their conversation. Mateship matters to Australians. Mates are there for you, watching your back and fighting your cause. Being an Australian comes with the entitlement of speaking one's truth. Caution needs to be exercised when asking an Australian their opinion since, without hesitation, they will be sure to tell you! There is never any intention to harm; it's simply, as an Australian would say, "Mind if I speak my mind mate?"

As I pondered Marilyn's offer, my fretful sleep patterns returned. I'd had two years to settle my emotions and get used to the bolts of grief which, without warning, would crash in on me. I was fearful of saying too much about my grief and risking reprimand from those impatient for me to be over it, to move on. So, in 2011, I did move on, in a different way. I would move on to Australia. Decision made.

* * *

I felt optimistic. Being back in Australia might be the reinvention I needed. As soon as I arrived, I addressed the logistics of finding a flat in the city near The Australian Ballet Centre and selling our home in Keilor. The house was too big for me, and too far out of the city. In any case, to be there without David was not something I could consider.

As I packed it up, I realised anew how much we'd travelled and where the past 30 years of our marriage had taken us. In addition to David's vast collection of antique ballet and theatre books collected from around the world, and his massive collection of Moorcroft pottery, there was our collection of antiques, each piece carefully chosen. We had shared a love of antiques and had adored spending afternoons searching for rare and interesting pieces together. There was a moment during the packing when our entire life together unfolded before me. Photographs, letters, ballet memorabilia, ballet posters from our touring days, gala invitations, receptions, our wedding, photos of us travelling the world, loving our jobs and each other. And so the boxes mounted. How wonderful the greater part of our life together had been.

David had left the book he'd been reading open on the kitchen table. I wept when I saw it. I desperately wanted him back.

Eventually, the house was empty and on the market. In Australia, once an offer is accepted it's only a matter of a few weeks before the deal is complete. One afternoon, I returned to the house and noticed someone had been sitting on our bed, probably gazing in awe at the glorious view into the nature reserve, as I'd done so many times. At that moment I knew the house had sold, gone out of my life. Before closing the door for the last time, I looked back, hardly recognising the home we'd made together. But I knew that the magnificent view down into the far-reaching nature reserve at the foot of our garden would never change, and I remember hoping the new owners would find as much joy in living there as we had found.

***

Finding a flat to rent near The Australian Ballet School studio was my next mission. I didn't want to be too far away from the centre of Melbourne, and preferably high up. A super flat appeared, and within days I'd moved in. I was impatient to get back to work, yet at the same time fearful of it. Would the familiar, creative woman I had been still be there for me? I panicked. Was returning to Australia a step too far? What if my grief was still too raw? Did I have the energy to front up and forge ahead?

The Australian Ballet School teachers and students were welcoming. I felt warmed and needed. Being around young talent was inspiring, and I knew I had to step up. The standard was high and the dancers in my care were fearless, ambitious young Aussies... a breed I knew well!

My apartment overlooked the Botanical Gardens, which I visited frequently. My weekends allowed long walks soaking up the Melbourne fresh air. But, as the months passed, I began to miss London, my spiritual home, the city where I felt embraced and which I loved in spite of its gloomy weather and endless inconvenience. I was finding it difficult to sit and rest, my urge to move was not subsiding; I could find no peace. David's love and enjoyment of living in Australia had given me pleasure. Without his encouragement to appreciate Australia I was lost.

I made up my mind to return to London.

* * *

I arrived back to my West London flat unsure of what I was going to do with the rest of my life. Gradually, I found my way back into the studio and managed to gather work. English National Ballet was just up the road in Kensington, and early coaching lessons with Ksenia Ovsyanick became my morning wake up. This became an enjoyable time. Being back in the studio distracted me from ruminating on concerns about my future.

I would fill the following years with more freelance work, taking English National Ballet School on tour with their educational programme *My First Ballet*. The tours were hectic. I was back on the road and enjoying being with fledgling dancers. Every summer, for the following seven years, I returned to my beloved Hydra. Arriving at the hotel each year without David was always my biggest dread. I felt lost and noticeably alone surrounded by couples and families. One year, my niece Carina flew from Australia to join me. Her visit was comforting, and we chatted for days, mulling over our lives and family issues.

And so, my life continued—a mixture of work, gallery visits, summers on the island and spending time with friends.

I'd given Australia a fair shot, and felt that returning to London had been the right decision. I continued my daily yoga practice, which had been part of my life for as long as I could remember. The simple positions allowed my body to stretch and relax, as well as giving me a feeling of taking care of myself.

As the years passed, I arrived at a point of acceptance. By then, David had been gone for seven years. He was not coming back. Though not totally free of longing for him, I was feeling a sense of peacefulness. My mind had calmed. I was able sleep well and concentrate long enough to get through a book. During that time I felt content being alone. Never once did I contemplate finding another relationship or person to love. I'd shut down the desire to feel loved. My life was compact. I'd regained strength, found my footing. I had dear friends whom I cherished. The family of Jeanetta Laurence, a Royal Ballet dancer who became the company's associate director, always invited me to their Christmas celebrations in Chiswick, never insisting but always lovingly leaving their door of friendship open to me. Other London friends stayed close, never failing to make contact. They kept a close eye on me, which was reassuring.

* * *

Each working year seemed to get longer, the gloomy London winters dragged, making the summer months ahead even more enticing. Cautiously, spring would show the first rays of sunshine, encouraging bursts of pale blue wisteria to cascade down the Victorian terraced houses in West London. With the arrival of spring, English people are quick to take off their clothes, impatient to grab a few rays of early sunlight on their milky white bodies. The Australian in me would think *why do they do this? It's not even warm!*

Finally, each summer, my travel day to Hydra would dawn. I'd be up at 5am to board my flight from Heathrow to Athens where I'd dash, with just moments to spare, out of the terminal. The scorching heat would hit me as I ran to catch the departing bus to Piraeus. Despite a tight travel timeframe from London to Athens, never once did I miss that bus, nor was my flight delayed. Finally, I'd board the JetCat, which would thunder its way through the torrid Aegean Sea, passing Poros and on to Hydra. As we'd turn the rocky corner and pass the National Merchant Marine Academy, the tiny Hydra port would come into view. And there they were: those familiar blue doors, shuttered windows, fishing boats, outdoor tavernas lining the port, and the promise of morning swims, dinner by the sea, lunch under grapevine canopies accompanied by a tipple of local wine. The blistering heat of each day would banish locals and well-worn visitors like myself to sleep in air-conditioned rooms, leaving on the streets only the unsuspecting tourists from the cruise ships, who splurged on mock-Greek knick-knacks as they sweltered beneath the midday sun.

My visit to the island in August 2017 was no different than my last seven visits. As always, I arrived alone, dragging my hand luggage up the little, windy street to my home away from home, the Bratsera Hotel. Feeling like a local, I chatted on the way to passers-by and marvelled at the heavily hampered donkeys carrying produce from the port to the tucked-away markets and stores. The donkeys' familiar clip clop spoke to their sure footedness on the slippery cobble stones. At Bratsera, I was greeted by Janice and the staff with the warmest welcome and hugs in true Greek style. My usual room, number 11, was waiting for me. Having returned to the island each summer after David's death, I was ready once more to languish, rejuvenate and, for a short time, immerse myself in a way of life I loved. With my London momentum halted, more than anything I just wanted to gaze uninterrupted at the hand-carved ceiling of my room.

My early morning swim would be followed by coffee at the port where I'd watch the local men unload produce that arrived overnight from Athens. I loved seeing the fishermen feeding scraps of food to the famous Greek cats who'd hover by the docks. I'd watch the waking sun move across the magnificent Academy of the Arts, which sat proudly on the hill opposite the port. Once the shadow of the sun passed the Academy, it was time to head back to Bratsera for breakfast.

Visits with my Russian family were never pre-planned. We'd meet by chance, or sometimes they'd come by the hotel to see if I happened to be about. On one such occasion Natasha, Lilly's daughter, found me taking a nap. I was thrilled to see her, and welcomed her into my room to take cover from the heat. How could we have known that this chance meeting was going to change my life?

Room 11 was cool, dark and soothing. The rhythm of the ceiling fan and earthy smell of the wicker grass matting on the floor made it a gentle nest, a welcome refuge from the heat outside. Soft white muslin curtains tumbled to the floor, covering the shuttered windows, and a deep red tapestry hung over the bed. The atmosphere was peaceful, and the perfect space for us to reconnect. Natasha and I perched on the end of the bed. We had much to catch up on.

Natasha was a child when we first met. Over the years she got to know Michael and especially David during those long summers. Like Lilly, her mother, Natasha's conversation is engaging and peppered with pearls of wisdom and a warm, lilting laugh. Her clipped English/Russian/Greek accent is coloured with a slightly throaty sound. We were in flow, meandering through memories, some of them dynamic, others heart-rending and mournful. I felt safe with Natasha; her mothering nature allowed me to express my grief and pain.

On this particular evening, in the safety of Natasha's company my heart burst open to her. I knew there were consequences of revealing one's deepest grief, but I went ahead anyway. The relief was enormous, but only momentarily as I was not prepared for what felt like her brutal response. "Petal," she said, "you come to the island for seven years as Petal the widow. Always the same: the widow, no change. It is time to open... open your heart, open everything please." I froze. I was offended, hurt and defensive. I remember saying, "Absolutely not, Natasha. I will open nothing." Natasha let my reply hang in the air. She was not going to rescue me. We moved out of my room into the garden. The impact of her chastening words remained. I would need to mull them over by myself.

I decided not to think about our conversation during the rest of my stay on the island, as I continued in my Greek routine: walking, reading and reliving lovely moments David and I had shared on the island over the years. We'd even flirted with the idea of buying a small bolt hole there. All we needed was a nest we could fall into each summer. But, as summers came and went, every year better than the one before, our days and weeks passed in the summer sunlight and we never got around to buying that nest.

* * *

When I arrived back in London the city was humid and hot. My freelance work had stacked up. In haste, I did my usual diary check, ticking off commitments already fulfilled. Looking forward to touring with English National Ballet graduates was at the top of my list. The dancers were talented and interesting young hopefuls. The provincial touring schedule looked relentless. However, it was broken up with periods in London where private coaching and mentoring gave me nourishing work to look forward to.

My conversation with Natasha continued to poke at me. I found myself chewing over her words, trying to understand exactly how they made me feel. The bad dreams returned. I wanted to talk about them in detail but stopped myself for fear of asking too much of my friends, as sharing vivid images from dreams about the gates of hell felt risky. I did not want to appear indulgent or wallowing, so I said nothing.

Nor did I allow myself to question why painful things happen. They happen.

That's all.

* * *

Free time on weekends allowed space for me to work through my life as it was. Couples holding hands began to register with me, especially those whose body language read *I'm part of you*. Such images were causing a distinct feeling of envy in me. Turns out I'd always loved being part of a couple. Fortunately, my being part of a couple had worked well with the men I'd married, since within that secure couple package came the acknowledgment of a freedom we both needed and cherished.

This new awareness of couples wrapped up in their togetherness came as a surprise. I was 69 years old, and since David's death I'd never considered looking at or imagined loving another man. Now, for the first time, I recognised it was tenderness I was missing, and I longed for it. My need to give and receive intimacy was catching up with me. I felt hollow, bereft of physical contact and the ecstatic exhaustion that followed. On the surface I was fine: my long-term mantra *get up, dress up and show up* never once let me down. I was good at it, due to years of practice as a ballet dancer. Unless bitten

175

by a tiger or abducted by a gang of thugs, no excuse would do. The show had to go on.

* * *

One evening, while having dinner and wine with my dear friend Mark Welford, he asked how I was feeling. I felt safe with Mark. We'd been through a lot together over the years, always there for each other, providing a soft place to fall if need be. Mark and Michael had been great friends, and shared a quick, cut-glass wit. The three of us had bonded as young dancers, sharing humour often not appreciated by others. Even when I was the butt of the banter I never failed to bite back! Our repartee got us through many hard times. So, when Mark asked how I was, I knew I could tell him the truth. "I feel shrivelled," I said. "I have no lustre and where the heck has my radiance gone?"

Mark called the following day. My words the previous night had concerned him. He said he could never think of me as shrivelled, and that word had unsettled him. There was nothing I could say. I was in a state of flux, unsure of exactly how to deal with what was dawning inside of me. Work continued and my dancers were making progress. I knew I was doing a good job. Yet my obsession with preparing them, with leaving no stone unturned, was obscuring things I needed to resolve. I felt impatient, anxious to understand and resolve the edginess that was overtaking me.

* * *

I decided to dig in and examine the cause of my unease. But where to start digging was the question. I told myself I was probably still in that weird grief place where lookalikes of people you've lost jump out at you, convincing you that you're seeing the person you miss, when you're merely seeing a similar head of hair, or a walk or a clothing style. Yet even those slightest resemblances ignite the pain all over again. When you lose someone you dearly love, everything becomes related to that feeling of loss. Paintings, books, theatre, music are all potential reminders of bereavement. And then there's the comments from others whose casual approach to something so painful could leave me choking down my screams. One acquaintance, shortly after David's death, said, "Life goes on dear Petal." I could only glare at her. "What makes you think I don't know that?" I asked.

I was acquainted with self-help books on co-dependency, grief, depression. In fact, I knew them so well I felt as though I'd invented them. The whole self-help bit of love-yourself-and-you-will-be-a-happy-person started in the '60s and continued on. Along with countless others I ate each one up, underlining certain sentences in case I needed reassurance, dog-earring pages, copying out personal reminders, all of them exhorting me to love myself. I ended up spending way too much money on these little books in the hope they held the answer to my hurt. You'd think, after all, that I'd know how to sort myself out. I didn't. So, while I stayed afloat and was never at a loss for something to do, I was far from feeling centred.

* * *

Jenni moved out of the flat next door. I was sad to see her go. She'd been such a help to me after David died. Tor, whom I imagine was in her late 30s at the time, moved into Jenni's flat; I liked her immediately. She seemed worldly, straightforward and blessed with a fun sense of humour. During her first summer we'd chat from time to time out on the deck, and on one particular day I asked how her online dating was progressing. She replied with little enthusiasm and then asked, "How's your life Petal? Are you dating online?"

Her tone was neutral, as if it were the most obvious question to ask. Pow! I felt out of step, outdated and bashful. I wasn't sure how to reply. Not wanting to sound too much like yesterday's news, I bumbled along saying I was 70 years old and how embarrassing it would be to advertise for company. Tor's response was instant. "But Petal," she said, "you're so cool."

I was chuffed. Me, cool? Never in my wildest dreams had I thought of myself as cool, but I sure as heck liked the sound of it. It occurred to me that Tor did not see me as "the widow", but then she and my other new young friends in the building had not known David.

* * *

Tor had touched a spark. I felt myself resisting her suggestion that I try online dating, but I was weakening to the idea. I remember feeling rather coquettish when I finally invited her to set me up on a dating website with one proviso: no one must know!

Tor asked if I would prefer a free or pay-to-join website? I could think of nothing more unattractive than a cheapskate male ogling my pics, so opted for a pay-to-join. We had fun selecting photographs. Not too skimpy, not sweet, not the elderly know-it-all matriarch and definitely no suggestion of ballet, which I presumed could be a turn-off to any prospective suitor. My biography kept rather a lot back. I settled on *70 years old, retired, interested in the arts and travel, no children, widowed, would like to meet person with similar interests preferably still involved in own career. No facial hair or beards please.* There. Done. I decided to take a random peep every so often for a laugh. I told myself this was not really me. I was a tiny bit ashamed to be searching publicly… for what?

Knowing no one knew what I was up to rather delighted me. I started to take a peep each night into the app, to see if any male had liked me. That one check became two, then three and, before I knew it, I was checking in during the day many times. I was on a roll and loving it.

My photographs were doing the job. Having been photographed hundreds of times as a dancer I knew the trick of choosing a good shot, at the same time being mindful not to deceive and lead some unsuspecting man up the garden path thinking he was getting a smooth-skinned 70-year-old who looks like a svelte 40-year-old. This rather bizarre journey had definitely begun to intrigue. I was captured, finding myself listing men with potential, encouraging each to divulge their story, which they seemed happy to do.

Yet how weird this all seemed. Men who are mostly shut down, reluctant to speak about their private lives, were online chatting away to a person they'd never met. I enjoyed teasing out their stories. Some were hilarious and became more and more fanciful as the conversation went on. Yachts, sports cars, holiday scenes, grandchildren, gardens; it was all there and mostly rather harmless. Retired accountants, vets, doctors, playwrights, artists—the list was endless. Men, all sounding rather happy with themselves. Invariably my pet dread would appear: photographs of men, who had seen the last of middle-age, done up in full-body cycling kit—helmet on top, flaunting Lycra head-to-toe, propped up against a bike... oh god my biggest turn off! Also, the wretched beard thing. Apparently, so many men have a fetish for facial hair. Did they not read my bio clearly stating NO facial hair or beards please! And then there were the occasions when the slip up would occur when, having spent some time exchanging messages, the hammer would fall: do you wear stockings or high heels? Delete! So funny! I'd laugh out loud thinking, *shame on you buddy you sounded okay for a split moment, but at least you revealed your game before wasting any more of my time.*

And so, the search continued. I felt better than I'd felt in a long time. At least I was doing something that could turn out to be positive and, even if not, the ride was giving me one hell of a laugh. Though there were some cheerless entries: men giving out unsparing private information driven by desperation in hope of finding a woman to be with, a woman to care for them, maybe even love. Many sounded careworn and dispirited. I was sobered by their heartbreaking honesty although, somehow, I knew better than to reach out to men who displayed too much neediness.

But after a few weeks I found that no one took my fancy. Some struck me as boring, over-sharing old gits running amuck with tribes of grandkids or launched into too many caravan holidays. I was feeling jaded, so decided to check in with Tor, who advised me to give it a break for a while.

* * *

Taking time out was not that easy. The thought of an irresistible, mature, matinee idol lurking there on the screen and waiting for me was an opportunity I did not want to miss. And there were other issues. I was not comfortable with feeling or appearing desperate which of course I was… desperate for affection and tenderness.

During my time out, questions plagued me. Was it my age that caused me to feel embarrassed and shameful? Was internet dating only for the young? Was I going to make a fool of myself? Well, no. At least not at this stage, because no one knew what I was playing at.

PART FOUR

SIMON

After one night I went back to the site. And then... Simon Winstanley popped up. He'd seen my picture, read my profile (skimpy as it was) and asked if it would be okay for him to email me.

Simon's profile was straight up. Working architect, four adult children, widower for three months, living in Scotland. I was sort of keen to chat with Simon, so I replied yes to his email. Simon's admission that his wife had died only three months previously tweaked my curiosity and seemed somehow brave. From his emails, I detected no pain or fear or self-recrimination. His honesty leapt out at me. We seemed to have a lot to chat about, as we touched on art, Scotland and places we'd visited. Simon said he was heading to Venice with his son for a few days. I mentioned that I had fond memories of Venice, especially the beautiful Teatro La Fenice. A few days later Simon emailed to tell me he was standing outside that theatre, that he'd explored its interior and yes it was very beautiful. I was liking the connection we were establishing.

Our emails became more and more frequent, going from one every few days to many times a day, often late into the night. We were starting to know about each other and enjoying the warm feelings we got through our writing. Early one evening Simon asked if he could give me his mobile number. He didn't want to impose himself upon me, he wrote, but he'd love to hear my voice sometime. I called him immediately. Over the years we laughed a lot when Simon would relive his astonishment and nervousness when his phone rang, and it was me.

His accent was English, soft and cultured with not a vestige of a Scottish brogue. Cautiously, not wanting to pry (Simon's words), he asked what my work or career had been. I told him I been a ballet dancer with the Sadler's Wells Royal Ballet, to which Simon replied, "I don't know much about ballet but I'm willing to learn."

I laughed out loud, delighted by his honesty, and assuring him that ballet was definitely not on my *have to know about* criteria. And so we graduated from emails to extended phone conversations day and night. On many evenings, Simon would talk me to sleep, my phone wedged between my pillow and my ear. I'd wake up with the phone on the floor and the battery dead. This went on for what seemed like weeks until Simon suggested we meet up for lunch in York. York was about halfway between London and his home in New Galloway and, since we'd discovered that we shared an interest in steam trains, while we were there we could visit the National Railway Museum.

I was very keen to meet Simon. He informed me that his plan was to book into a hotel, as the drive back to his home from York was long and it was safer to stay over. This left me wondering. What if our trip to the museum and our lunch following it extended and I missed my train back to London? I surely did not want to be at Simon's mercy with nowhere to stay. So, to be sensible and safe, I booked a room for myself in the same hotel. I decided to arrive there the day before we would meet, which would allow me to feel less nervous and to take time dolling myself up! It had been ages since I'd bothered with my wardrobe.

The days before our planned meeting were filled with excitement and sleepless nights. I couldn't wait to meet this lovely man. He'd not said one awkward, insensitive or off-putting word during our many conversations. Each time we spoke I felt warmth and affection coming from him… I was a goner. This was a gigantic step for me. What on earth was I doing? But the unknown was thrilling. For the first time in years I felt light and happy.

* * *

The day I'd booked to travel to York finally dawned. I enjoyed the train journey, checked into my room, had a good night's sleep, woke with the sparrows, and was dressed and in the lobby waiting for Simon to arrive at 11am. I saw a car pull in, and the man who got out of this car wore subtle, elegant clothing and had a gentle, round face. It was absolutely Simon. For a moment I watched him as he walked toward the hotel's front door. I remember running towards him, arms outstretched, then feeling Simon wrap his arms around me, holding me very close for the longest time.

That afternoon we walked by the river talking incessantly, tingling with delirium and fluster. Even though we'd spent so much time emailing and talking throughout the previous three weeks we couldn't stop explaining our past lives and exchanging thoughts. Late that afternoon, wandering back to the hotel, Simon suddenly wrapped me into his arms again, and said he was in love with me. I did not question his statement. I absolutely knew it to be true. I also knew I loved Simon from the moment he held me that morning.

That weekend, we didn't manage a visit to the National Railway Museum nor did Simon get to use his room! Before we met, my thoughts had been crazed with premature imaginings. What if we were to sleep together? Would my body remember how to react, would I have to block out feeling embarrassed, would sleeping with Simon so soon be a step too far? In Simon's hands, as he made love to me, I need not have worried. He cradled me gently, engendering feelings I knew I never wanted to live without.

We parted tearfully, with Simon pleading with me to visit his home in Scotland the following weekend. At that moment I'd have driven to Timbuktu had he asked me. The week dragged; we were desperate for each other. Even our long day and night phone calls brought no satisfaction or relief from our longing.

* * *

Being back in London gave me time to think about what was happening to me, and between us. At 70 years of age, we had fallen hopelessly in love… how utterly outrageous, invigorating and unexpected was this? I felt hypnotised from the moment Simon kissed me. He was compelling, and beautiful and I couldn't get enough of him.

Two weeks previously, I'd confided to Mark and Rachel that I was playing around on a dating website. I had needed their support, and enjoyed their sharing in my mischievous undercover search. We'd laughed a lot at the expense of desperate males on the lookout for a companion. Both Mark and Rachel were tickled when I shared the extent of my York weekend, though they were a wee bit surprised at my adventurousness. When I told Mark I was going to Simon's house somewhere in Scotland the following weekend he went into shock horror overdrive. "You don't know this man!" he exclaimed, "He could be a rapist, a murderer! You don't even know where he lives and you've agreed to go to his house somewhere in the wilderness on a mountain in Scotland! NO!" Nothing I said could appease Mark's fears for my safety. Once he realised my mind was made up, his rant continued. He also looked up Simon's website and insisted that I give him Simon's phone number along with his car registration as soon as he collected me in Carlisle. Step-by-step text messages to him were also on the to-do list! Rachel, excited at my breakthrough, was nonetheless apprehensive about the remote location of Simon's home. Even so, though I knew she shared Mark's concerns, her sisterly support held strong. And I had no doubts about my safety in going to Simon's home.

* * *

Simon greeted me at Carlisle station with open arms, packing me tightly next to him in the car as he drove through New Galloway with one hand on the wheel and the other feeling for my hand; something he always did when driving, much to my apprehension. His house was stunning; he called it The Houl. This beautiful space Simon created was much like creating a ballet. Just as choreography requires attention to every step, every inch of the house had been carefully crafted with attention to each detail. Its position on its remote site was chosen to capture sunlight and space. On entering the house one was not prepared for the magnificent landscape visible behind great walls of glass. Every massive window allowed the panorama to seep into the house, bathing it in light and warmth.

When Simon first invited me to his home one of my first questions had been, "Do you have heating?" With one of his funny chuckles, he would often remind me of that. What I quickly discovered was that Simon had seen to everything and anything that could enhance one's comfort. There were no dark, damp, mouldy patches to cringe away from. Scandinavian double-glazed windows and doors and under-floor heating in every room kept the cold at bay. The house was sealed, and air ventilated throughout, which made it a cosseting place to be. I was sold on living in a zero-carbon house, although the technology was baffling. Simon the trailblazer had introduced sustainable living from the start of his architectural practice in 1983, believing that buildings should create their own energy from locally available renewable energy sources. He strove to produce buildings that would brighten their dwellers' emotional and physical responses to the places where they lived, worked and socialised. I never had the urge to rearrange a piece of furniture or a painting or an object; I was in total harmony with the layout and contents of his home. I could see no evidence of anyone having lived in that house other than Simon. It was his creation, his landmark, which I loved and adored. He often reminded me the house was mine to share and do with whatever I wanted. But I wanted nothing more or different. I felt sheltered and at peace.

The experience of being in a snow-covered, freezing cold land while living in a toasty house was utter bliss for a cold frog like me. This house was not only graceful and beauteous, it was utterly functional in every possible way. I would especially relish being able to stroll, scantily clad, about the house and still feel warm. In Simon's house I would always feel relaxed, cocooned, safe and needed. His intention, as he explained it, had been to build a home for him and his wife to retire to, a place to relax and enjoy family and grandchildren. He'd briefly outlined his children's lives and offered brief words about his late wife, saying she'd been unwell for some time and had died unexpectedly after a major operation. Clearly the designing and building of this home was dear to his heart, and he was quietly proud of it. At that stage I knew very little of Simon's professional accolades. Self-promotion was not in his character; only in time would I discover for myself the wealth of his highly recognised and respected achievements.

* * *

Once we were inside The Houl, Simon opened a bottle of champagne—a delightful prologue before we melted into each other. I remember burying my face in his neck, loving the softness of his skin and the gentle sound of his breath.

Our first night together at The Houl was wonderfully long. We woke in the darkness holding onto each other, made love and drifted back to sleep, entwined. I remember waking up to Simon stroking my hair and sensing the aroma of freshly brewed coffee, toast and homemade jam. And thinking *what on earth am I doing?* I had no answer. I was bereft of reason and in a state of euphoria beyond my control. Here I was in a strange house, miles from London, being made love to passionately. How did this happen? All I knew was that I was helpless to resist. Simon had grabbed hold of every bit of me and was not letting go. We spent the weekend in our dressing gowns getting to know each other in safety and calmness. By the time I needed to head back to London, Simon had asked me to move into The Houl with him. I had no doubt that I would do precisely that, but there were issues to be resolved. We were both working, though retirement was looming; therefore, travel to and from Scotland would be needed. At least for a while.

* * *

During the following six weeks we devoted our weekends to being together, either in Scotland or at my flat in London. I had not yet divulged my new life to friends, as I was way too exhilarated to make any sense. Also, I was enjoying having a private life and felt no need to share it with anyone except Mark and Rachel, both of whom, by then, were fully supportive. But I pondered how my other friends might respond to this new set of circumstances I was in. If I told them I had fallen in love at 70 years of age with a man who lived in the wilderness of Scotland would they question my sanity? Would my union with Simon be seen as a betrayal of David? To me the situation felt natural and necessary if I were to continue my search for a nourishing life. So I quickly stopped worrying about what certain friends might make of it. I knew what I was doing, and why.

That we had met on the internet was another confession I was dreading. Would it be seen as unbecoming and uncouth at my stage of life? I knew I had to stop overthinking. I'd found love and tenderness from a man who showed concern for me. Each caress Simon laid upon me was confirmation of his love and desire for me. Weekends spent at The Houl were easy and comfortable. We slid gently into each other's ways.

Life found its own gentle rhythm. I was comfortable with our arrangement, managing to juggle London work with weekends in Scotland, and enjoying the journey from Euston to Dumfries on Friday afternoons, when I would be brimming with excitement at the thought of spending nights wrapped in Simon's arms. We frequently grabbed opportunities to travel, spending weekends in Paris, Florence and Berlin, where Simon introduced me to how buildings were thought out, structured, styled and the intention of the architect. I loved being with him. His never needing to grandstand or convince anyone of his cleverness was intensely attractive to me; a trait I knew and had loved in David.

* * *

I had told Simon of my love for Greece and, when I said I would be booking my usual summer holiday to my beloved island Hydra, Simon asked, without hesitation, if he could join me. Thrilled by the idea of a lengthy holiday together we set our plans in motion and took off. I'd reminisced rather a lot to Simon, explaining my years on the island, and he was enchanted and keen to know the island and my friends.

We were joyfully welcomed at Bratsera Hotel by Janice and the staff. Arriving with Simon I felt dizzily happy once again. I was part of a couple, no longer alone. Room 11 was waiting for us, cool and inviting. It had been a long day of travel. Though we were flagging we took an evening stroll by the port; something I'd done so many times and wanted to share with him. Our days were filled with early morning swims, followed by coffee at the port, where Simon shared in my joy at watching the sun rise across the School of Fine Arts. Then back to the hotel for a super slap-up breakfast. The rest of the day would be spent walking, reading, chatting with friends, lunch followed by long afternoon sleeps escaping the heat of the day. We were blissfully loving to each other.

I had spoken openly about my previous life to Simon, detailing my marriage of 30 years to David and my marriage to Michael. I'd explained how David and I had thrived during our long working partnership, which entailed being together 24 hours a day for 16 years, first in Sadler's Wells Royal Ballet followed by The Australian Ballet. Simon was intrigued. He questioned how we'd remained attracted to and interested in each other when being at such close range for so long. I explained that, within the ballet world, dancing, working and living together was not uncommon and that when I was dancing marriage to someone outside that world would not have worked for me.

Simon had not divulged much about his marriage, and I knew better than to pry. After all, his wife had died only three months before we met, and it seemed right that he protect himself from intrusive questions. I did know that his father had died in an aircraft accident when Simon was a few months old and that, as an only child, his mother had sent him to boarding school when he was six. He believed his mother thought she was doing the best for him, and maybe that was the case. He held no grudge towards her, but repeatedly told me how homesick he had been, how sad and frightened and alone he felt as a small, shy boy. As he opened his heart to me, his tears would fall. I found these disclosures unspeakably sad. A six-year-old sent away with no loving arms to run to upset me terribly. I once told Simon that I knew that little boy; I'd seen his face on a few occasions and understood what those sad eyes were saying. Had my mother sent me away I'd have taken her to task needing to know how the hell she could have done that to me. Was it an easy way out or was it a case of sheer necessity? Either way, Simon had lived without parental love from age six. It occurred to me that there were similarities between Simon and David's childhoods. Both yearned for more motherly love than they received, and that had left its mark.

Putting together the threads of Simon's life, a picture was emerging that I sensed was far from complete. His urgent neediness for me was impossible to ignore. Simon was in a state of love famine, which had left him with a hungering for affection, attention and tenderness from me every moment of the day. It seemed he'd found safety in our relationship, which allowed him to speak his truth and be listened to. Yet I sensed a lack of trust on his part, and when I asked him about it, as gently as I could, a few days passed before he was able to reply. Then, with a timid, wobbly voice he told me he'd once been betrayed and deeply hurt—something he could never deal with again, and which made the possibility of losing me unimaginable. His tears flowed and, for a few moments, I saw again the face of that abandoned little boy. Moving into Simon's arms I held him for the longest time, reassuring him of my love and devotion to our life together.

Simon's vulnerability prompted questions in my mind. How could such a bruising betrayal happen to this kind, trustworthy, loving human being? My heart broke as I tried to imagine what it must feel like to grapple with such a terrible fear of abandonment. Simon deserved to feel at peace, and my desire to protect him was mounting. It didn't take long for him to feel secure in my love... he'd found a safe place and he knew it.

We had had a wonderful holiday. Simon was taken with the island and shared my love of its beauty. He was eager to plan a return visit, and even suggested we consider buying a studio there. Natasha and my Russian/Greek family were overjoyed that I'd found love and was no longer the solitary widow. Little did Natasha know then that it was her conversation with me that night at the Bratsera Hotel that had been the spark that enabled me to reinvent myself, open my heart and invite love in. I would tell her this, but later.

* * *

Back in London, I informed English National Ballet School management I'd be bringing a friend the following day to watch a rehearsal. Simon was in awe of the dancers, and apparently of me! The next day our wonderful stage manager Sarah-Jayne Powell who'd been at the rehearsal said to me, "What's with the twinkle between you and that guy yesterday?"

I was tickled. Here were Simon and I thinking we were the coolest adults on the planet giving nothing away of our secret love affair. I said nothing, but Sarah-Jayne knew the answer to her question. She was the first to catch the love glow between us. Her sheer delight and happiness for us was more than encouraging, coming as it did with approval and joy at our finding love.

I decided to share my news with two dear friends, who were surprised and delighted, asking questions about Simon and wanting to know how we met. They were not fazed when I told them we'd met on the internet, and instead praised me for my bravery. Thus far my story had been received with support and affection—so far so good! I was gaining confidence and, in any case, I was blinded by love and lust and caring less and less about how others might perceive my new life.

One day I met with a very good friend, Samira Saidi, known as Sami—a former dancer with Sadler's Wells Royal Ballet and later Director of Dance at English National Ballet School. I couldn't wait to tell her my news. She listened quietly. Her face did not express joy for me but bewilderment at what I was telling her. Without reservation she expressed concern that I was diving so deliberately and deeply into a relationship with a man newly widowed. Was he going to use me to get him through his sadness? And then what? I sensed no amount of convincing was going to ease her worries and, although she had rather burst my bubble, I respected her opinion and was touched by her straight talking. By the time we parted that day, she was suggesting I slow down, and I was as determined as ever to charge ahead come what may. Over the years I've confessed to Sami how much her care for me at that time meant, and we've remained true and devoted friends.

* * *

As the weeks passed, Simon was increasingly dissatisfied with our living arrangements. He said the many days apart were not working for him, and that he wanted to be with me permanently. The only way this could happen was if I stopped working. But what if I stepped away from my work and hated living in Scotland? I'd have lost my place in the work chain, which was already overrun by younger teachers, and any hope of retrieving my place seemed unlikely. Would living without my daily creative hit unleash anguish and regret? Was it too much to ask of my body and emotions? Could I walk away from the sensation I'd sought and thrived on all my life? Could I let go of my pillar of support? Would Scotland and Simon's love be enough to sustain a new life far from the womb of my creative world? Many friends questioned why on earth I was even considering this.

One thing that troubled me, as I fantasised about my future with Simon, was whether I was casting a heavy burden on him. Was I hoping he would replace what I might miss of my life in London? I was wavering, hankering for attachment but wary of giving up my ballet life and expecting Simon to complete my existence. I needed to process this move carefully. The potential for hurt and breaking this kind, loving man was a responsibility that weighed on me. Yet I also could not deny that the lust we shared was intoxicating. Nor could I escape the chemistry between us, and the realisation that it would not subside. Beyond that, I was swept up by Simon's delight at the prospect of our living together. He'd already set in motion the process that would secure his retirement. We both wanted to give our relationship a fair shot and were keen to get on with it, knowing time was not on our side. And so I headed full-on into my life with Simon. I knew our relationship deserved all the time, love and care I could muster, providing it was what I wanted more than anything. And it was. The burden of ambition was gone. I was free.

* * *

At last, we were living together at The Houl, spending time walking, cooking, learning about each other's past lives and listening to Simon's vast collection of jazz and classical music. Jazz had never been part of my musical vocabulary until each evening, while preparing our meal, Simon would present me with a glass of wine and background jazz music of his liking, which soon became my liking. Living in Scotland in a beautiful but remote property was nothing like my busy London life. In the beginning, I felt the distinct lack of choices Scotland had on offer. Things I was accustomed to – among them going to impromptu theatre performances and galleries, and travel opportunities direct from Heathrow – were not on the menu. But walking, driving and drinking up the landscape pacified my wanderlust, and I adapted quickly to life away from London. We were together, enjoying each moment, and looking forward to continuing our life journey.

Weekend stayovers at The Houl were always colourful. We were joined for an hilarious weekend by my dear friend Britt Tajet-Foxell – who had been the company's physiotherapist at Sadler's Wells Royal Ballet – along with her husband, Peter Bourke, a Shakespearean actor. Tripping down memory lane, we laughed a lot during evenings enhanced by pink champagne and chocolate truffles. Peter and Simon got on famously, and would pass the hours speaking of theatre, art and architecture with oodles of laughs thrown in, while Britt and I curled up on the sofa in our red tracksuits remembering our touring days in long, heartfelt chats.

I enjoyed introducing Simon to composers who were new to him, among them Malcolm Arnold, Max Richter, Arvo Pärt. Together we'd listen to Bach, Shostakovich, Sibelius, Vivaldi. Simon would ask me to explain how it felt to dance to Shostakovich and especially to Stravinsky. I saw how intensely interested he was by the ways in which music and the filigree of ballet steps fitted together. He was not surprised when I told him today's choreographers were using architects to design their sets. This made perfect sense to him. I remember telling him how one of the choreographers I most admire, Wayne McGregor, had used an architect to design *Chroma*, a ballet he made for The Royal Ballet, saying, "It's odd as there appears to be no scenery."

Simon, knowing exactly which architect could be that minimalistic, responded "That would be the architect John Pawson."

When we watched the ballet online, he said, "There is scenery, it's just not in the way."

Simon then took me to visit the Design Museum in Kensington designed by John Pawson and I fell in love with Pawson's work. The museum became one of our favourite London haunts. We had much to share during the coming years, getting to know each other's past and planning our future. We were engrossed in finding out about our respective passions, ballet and architecture. Simon's observation was that ballet and architecture are entwined, in that both require attention to detail and focus along with a good dose of curiosity and addiction, which make them pretty much a perfect match.

In time I came to understand Simon's passion for designing sustainable buildings. Doing so had won him many design awards, including one, in 2011, from the Royal Institute of British Architects (RIBA) for The Houl. But, while sustainability and energy efficiency were important to him, architecture and design always came first. Because he had been a tutor at the famous Mackintosh School of Architecture we had much to discuss about teasing out talent and developing students. He believed, and I agreed, that we all have potential in varying degrees, but that potential alone is not enough. Producing the finest work requires commitment, curiosity, grit and passion.

At times, Simon would ponder on how our lives might have been had we met during the '60s and early '70s when we were both working in Covent Garden. When in London we'd stroll down Floral Street next to the Royal Opera House and imagine we were meeting there for the first time. Simon's take was that I would never have fancied him as he was always the shy one at the back of the crowd. "Wrong, Simon!" I laughingly told him. "The quiet ones were the ones I went for. I'd have snapped you up!"

* * *

We had been living together for a while when, to my surprise, Christopher Powney, Artistic Director of The Royal Ballet School, asked if I would consider choreographing a ballet for the students. I hesitated, but only slightly, knowing the work would involve possibly six weeks rather than years, and Simon was up for it. As I began my work, I could see that Simon took a genuine interest in it. I appreciated that he was eager to learn about it yet never pushed to be included. At one point, I was given permission for him to attend rehearsals. Even though I assured him it would be fine for him to do something else, he attended every rehearsal over many weeks, fascinated by the construction of the work, and devoted to supporting me. Much of my planning took place during weekends at The Houl where, in the beautiful living area, I would spend endless hours jumping up and down as I worked out suitable steps and sequences, while Simon read his newspaper and asked occasional questions.

I valued his input while selecting my music. His vast knowledge of classical music was helpful. Working though the music for a new ballet is tedious, requiring weeks of putting the pieces together followed by continual rearranging until the choreographer knows everything fits. Having witnessed all my pre-studio planning, he was captivated when he watched me work with the dancers and link them with the choreography and the music. "It's taking shape," he exclaimed, "and, more importantly, it makes total sense." I loved having him in the studio and sharing my other love with him.

On one of our London weekends, I decided to take him to a ballet performance at the Linbury Theatre at the Royal Opera House. Alessandra Ferri, a consummate ballerina and artist who is always an inspiration to me, was presenting a bijou entitled *Trio ConcertDance*—a specially choreographed evening of dancing with her partner, the virtuoso Herman Cornejo, accompanied by a pianist. I could not wait to see the show, though I was unsure as to whether Simon would enjoy an evening of contemporary ballet. My concerns were unfounded. At the end of the performance Simon turned to me saying "Darling, now I see why you love your work so much."

I was enamoured of his work too, and burst with enthusiasm as I learned about buildings and the work of specific architects like the Australian Glen Murcutt, who creates environmentally responsible buildings rooted in the climate and tradition of Australia. Then there was David Chipperfield, a British architect who designed the monumental Neues Museum in Berlin. The Isokon building in Camden's Belsize Park spiked a special interest in me as it is a perfect example of Brutalist architecture. The style of the early 20th century Modernist movement also drew me in. Le Corbusier designs entered my life along with the simplicity of Scandinavian minimalist furnishings by Fritz Hansen, Arne Jacobsen, Alvar Alto and the Hungarian architect and furniture designer Marcel Breuer. Having lived with a collector I embraced my introduction to the

world of minimalism with gusto, and to this day have not
let go.

* * *

We made the most of our occasional trips to London, where
we were often en route to one of our chosen European cities
or simply enjoying a London fix catching up with theatre,
galleries, concerts. During the summer of 2019 we visited
Oslo. Some of my former students were dancing with the
Norwegian National Ballet; I looked forward to connecting
with them, and I was keen to share with Simon the beauty of
the Oslo Opera House, designed by the forward-thinking
architectural firm Snøhetta.

The Oslo Opera House remains one of my most loved
buildings. Arriving at the foot of it we stood holding hands for
the longest time. We were silent and breathless as we gazed at
what seemed like a magnificent iceberg floating toward us.
The building is a temple, a place of wonder portraying slender,
cool elegance on the outside while being warm, cosseting
and quiet inside. The womb of this noble building contains
a splendid ballet company, which performs classical and
contemporary work. We spent a day in one of the enormous
studios watching the dancers rehearse. The studio had been
designed with one wall of glass capturing the most glorious
landscape. The dancers gave us an affectionate welcome; I was
touched that they were thrilled to see me, and to meet Simon.
As the day moved on one of the dancers I'd taught, Douwe
Dekkers, invited us to watch his rehearsal of a section from the
ballet *Carmen*. His portrayal of Don Juan was deeply moving,
so much so that Simon and I were in tears by the end. The
reward of seeing my former pupil cross the threshold from
dutiful student to seasoned, sensitive performer came as a
quiet reminder that, just maybe, my input may have

contributed to what we were watching. As I later explained to Simon, the giant step from student to professional into a heritage tradition is a daunting prospect for every hopeful dancer. The dream is just beginning; there are no guarantees.

* * *

Simon, like David, was a dedicated petrol head. Both of them, having owned many cars from a young age and being forever fascinated by anything on wheels, treated themselves to vintage vehicles with great pride and exhilaration. At one point, Simon surprised me with an open-top classic, vintage Porsche—a present for us both in celebration of his retirement and our life together. I was horrified, having already experienced David's white Toyota MR2 matchbox, which played havoc on my abdominal muscles and my back to say nothing of clambering ungracefully in and out of the wretched thing. And now, I thought, once again I'll be begging my body to tolerate another uncomfortable antique relic on wheels. Simon's plan was to drive me around Scotland the following summer, the islands of Eigg, Harris, Skye all on the list. So we headed off, with the roof down and me with my Grace Kelly head scarf, Simon smiling from ear to ear and "All You Need Is Love" blaring from crackly old CD player. Simon was a speedy driver, always foot down, which scared me a bit. Behind the wheel, Simon was a devil in heaven. He'd glow as we'd duck and dive our way through the Scottish countryside, driving for miles, soaking up the landscape and booking into various hotels. Each evening we'd enjoy a meal followed by making love till dawn. Beneath Simon's quiet exterior lay a passionate and ardent lover. I remember my body feeling wholly desirable and smothered in love. Each night I clung to him, loving the sound of his breath, not wanting him to sleep and drift away from me. That sobering, yet realistic sense we'd had from the

199

beginning – that time was not on our side – intensified our urgent appetite for each other. Perhaps we were intuiting that something unforeseen might wrench us apart.

* * *

Into the second year of our relationship Simon asked if we should consider upgrading the London flat. I was surprised as I thought it was serviceable, central, with a nice view of London from the eighth floor. What was the need to change? Simon persisted, saying he'd like to make the flat more comfortable for us, opening up the living area, bringing in more light. After some thought I told him to go ahead and do whatever he thought best, at which point he asked me for a brief. I responded: warmth, light, warm woodwork and a soft glow to escape the gloominess of London. Soon, the ceiling and walls had come down, the flat was gutted and Simon was in full flight. I looked on, with absolute trust in his taste and style. But, inevitably, the renovation generated a good deal of angst. Construction mistakes were picked up on by Simon's meticulous architect's eye. For me, having my own architect on site was pure joy, though this was not quite the case for the builders. They knew Simon was watching over the quality of their workmanship and scrutinising every detail. A year later the work was complete—we settled in to a flat he had transformed into a beautiful, open, calm retreat. Life was ideal.

* * *

Initially, I was regarded with curiosity and trepidation by the locals in Simon's New Galloway hamlet of Kendoon, and by residents of nearby Castle Douglas, where our village High Street was located. Simon was keen to integrate me into the community, though I anticipated the possibility of a negative reaction to my living at The Houl. I did my best to engage with neighbours and locals. However, resentment towards me did not take long to surface. Soon, my dreams of acquiring a new-found, gentle country life began to fade. As a teacher and professional working woman I had mixed successfully with all ages and cultures. I was deflated by being blatantly ignored or met with cool indifference, but Simon was hopeful that, in time, a level of understanding and acceptance would be reached. Instead, I quickly learned that entering village life is not for the faint hearted. I was going to need emotional stamina and the skin of a rhinoceros. What didn't these village folk understand? Surely Simon had a right to live free from judgement. The least I had hoped for was a general appreciation that he was happy, no longer alone but loved and cared for. Yet the local community had no qualms about showing their disapproval of our relationship. Whatever friendly move I made was met with resistance. There was a kind of tribal unity, a group mindset that had made it acceptable to vilify me. It was horrible.

I felt embarrassed by the villagers' rudeness and found myself wondering exactly what lay beneath it. There was definitely an air of *burn her at the stake* eeriness, and I occasionally sought momentary amusement by imagining a scenario in which I was barefooted, with flowing hair and a billowing floor-length skirt and rope-bound wrists, as I was chased by the crowd up the High Street to the clock tower, to be greeted by a pack of Scottish dogs and a pile of fire-ready twigs!

Inevitably, my reception in the community made for an increasingly stressful time and often plummeted me into sadness. I felt powerless, and suggested to Simon that, as there was no sign of our relationship being accepted by the village folk, perhaps we should consider separating. Simon would hear none of it and so we rode the waves together.

* * *

Despite what greeted me in the village, living at The Houl was nurturing. It was more like a health retreat than a house. Every day the rooms would fill with sunshine from sunup till dusk. Nothing could hide from the summer light, which would filter into the house, causing rays to shimmer on small, elegant objects Simon had carefully placed in the living area.

We were happy and deeply in love enjoying time together, taking each day as it presented itself. I was learning to adapt to a slower pace of life, and paying attention to our health and well-being. Springtime filled me with curiosity. There was always something new happening on the farms around the property. A new experience was watching baby lambs struggle onto their feet, and once or twice I'd watched the miracle of birth, seeing the just-born baby lambs being licked and comforted by the mother ewe.

The distinct opposite of that magical experience came each year before Christmas, when I heard the heartbreaking cries of cows during the night as farmers took away their calves who would be slaughtered and sold as veal. Their cries tortured me. I hated it, and it greatly diminished my affection for farmers and farming. Simon's explanation in defence of the farming community made no difference. I found it loathsome, beastly and cruel. I cared deeply about animals of every breed. Especially dogs. Simon, it turned out, had never owned a dog and was somewhat indifferent to them. Nonetheless, he agreed to adopt a tiny black and tan Cavalier King Charles Spaniel. We named him Winston. To my delight, it only took a moment for Simon and Winston to become inseparable. They would sit together, with Winston on Simon's knee, or they'd lie side-by-side having a nap, their soft snoring pleasing to my ear. Winston completed our family. For a retired couple living on a large property in Scotland, I often thought, what could be more perfect?

* * *

Because Simon had decided to retire we needed to dismantle his office on the large top floor, a space he owned. This was a mammoth task of back-breaking work, as we were faced with disposing of 30 years of office equipment and documentation. We took it slowly, and at times I wondered if we would ever get to the bottom of it. By mid-November 2019 the weather had plummeted into the depths of a bleak, glacial Scottish winter. We knew we had to plough ahead at his office despite treacherous, icy roads, as he was keen to empty it and get the property on the market. Our compatible attention to detail pushed us forward. Simon loved my discipline when a job had to be done, and together the architect and ballet minds became one.

There was a lot to be sorted. Each day we'd drive to the office, giving ourselves an allocated time to work on a particular task. I understood when Simon had moments of poignant recollection; I'd witnessed similar emotions when I'd supported David through his retirement and subsequent grief, Simon's sense of loss was not new to me. But I could see that the workload was taking a toll on him, and he'd frequently become overwhelmed by the enormity of the job.

In January and February we tried to push ahead. I'd pack a thermos of coffee and sandwiches to see us through till the afternoon, but we were fading. Travelling in the freezing cold to and from the office each day was becoming more and more stressful and exhausting, and even after hours of hard slog we seemed to be getting nowhere. Simon was not coping. He'd become vague and sometimes frozen, unable to move or tell me what was wrong. I put these episodes down to stress, exhaustion and sadness in parting with his lifelong business.

He had started asking me to address his letters, saying his eyes were playing up. He was also showing a lack of spatial awareness when driving. There were many near misses, so many that I became afraid when in the car with him. Equally concerning was that he'd developed a weird facial expression which I could not define. There was a blankness, and he would be devoid of expression even when we'd be laughing at something on television. Initially I'd tease him saying, "You've got that funny face on darling." He'd reply, "Which one?" And we'd laugh. But we could not keep making light of it. Clearly, an appointment with his GP was in order. The doctor's assessment was that Simon was under stress and exhausted. He prescribed antidepressants. I was concerned there was more to Simon's strangeness than overload from clearing the office. My sense of alarm rose as I sensed he was spiralling beyond my grasp.

By this time, I was thrashing around doing my best to see beyond the mess, and Simon was mostly detached and mentally muddled. We had no idea about to what to do about the mountain of work ahead. Not knowing how to grapple with it, I asked a local antique dealer, Jason Burford, to take a look at the remaining debris thinking that maybe a sale would get rid of it. In a lucid moment, Simon asked Jason if he would completely dispose of the office machinery and debris, of which there was tons. Jason said he would, and I thanked my guardian angel. We'd been rescued. Over the next two weeks Jason and his team cleared the office completely, delivering bits to Simon at the house, taking a load to the Glasgow auction house, and cleaning the office top to bottom. Yet Simon was getting worse, and the antidepressants were doing no good. The rough winter weather was creating potholes in the road up to the house, making it impossible to drive. Again, Jason came to our rescue. On seeing the dangerous state of the track, he arrived the next day and filled in the potholes so I could get up to the house in the car without struggling on ice and rubble.

And then, suddenly, we went into the first weeks of the Covid-19 lockdown.

* * *

We were well-versed in Covid rules and regulations; however, as our government appeared not too concerned, we felt a few weeks in lockdown would be easy to handle. A warm home, beautiful views, music and food delivery made it not a big ask, and we had each other. On thinking back, we were just a tiny bit smug. Friends in London seemed to be having a harder time with the city closing down and working from home gathering momentum. Our life had not really changed too much, other than cutting back on weekends away. I spent time mentoring dancers by phone, supporting their hopes and encouraging positive thoughts, though later I would come to doubt the usefulness of conjuring up relentless encouragement when the truth was that we had no idea when life would return to normal.

As the weeks passed, lockdown was extended, travel rules were introduced, and Simon's symptoms became more noticeable. He was unsteady on his feet and finding it difficult to dress himself. Watching him try to undo his shirt and get out of his trousers confirmed that whatever was happening to him was more than stress and fatigue. By this time, doctor's appointments were strictly by phone and, despite my persistence, we could get neither a face-to-face appointment nor an answer to what was happening.

Around this time, Simon designed a play pen for our new little pup, so that Winston could learn to dash outside when needed and have a safe outdoor area to play. But the builders who'd been engaged to erect the fenced perimeter were surprised and puzzled when some of Simon's measurements failed to tally. To make it work, they altered the design, which caused Simon extreme embarrassment and frustration. This was one of many early realisations for Simon that skills he had possessed throughout his life were fading from his mind, and it produced a day of sadness I will never forget.

* * *

Without satisfactory answers or a diagnosis, we were locked into what felt like a state of madness. Simon had started experiencing frozen episodes, during which he'd appear to be stuck physically and mentally for some time. This was another frightening symptom which bothered me. He could not explain what it felt like, nor did he seem to know when it was happening.

I continued to persist with our GP, asking for another opinion. Weeks later, an appointment was made for us to visit an NHS neurologist in Dumfries & Galloway Infirmary, but it would not take place for another eight weeks. In a fit of frustration and fear I called a random neurologist in Glasgow, begging for a private consultation regardless of the cost. With lockdown at its peak, the possibility of a face-to-face doctor's appointment anywhere in the United Kingdom was as unlikely as being bitten by a tiger snake. I must have sounded desperate—enough that we were granted an appointment in Glasgow for the following week. In the interim, endless Covid instructions for face-to-face appointments arrived by email.

Finally, the day of the appointment arrived. The bitterly cold weather had left thick ice covering the roads, and warnings were issued not to drive due to hazardous conditions. Normally we wouldn't have contemplated driving anywhere, but we had to get answers, and treatment. I packed water and a food hamper for Simon and myself and made a warm nest for our little Winston in the back of the car. Knowing we'd have to leave him there while we saw the doctor, I'd fortified the nest with thermal blankets, two hot water bottles and dressed him in his little thermal coat. It had to be enough for that half hour we would be inside the hospital.

Due to lockdown, the reception area was dark and empty, other than a woman hidden behind a mask and a glass panel. At first, she was not pleased that I was in the building but, realising Simon was unsteady and unresponsive, she agreed that, as his carer, I needed to accompany him into the doctor's very large, bleak room.

The doctor immediately commenced asking Simon questions. He answered some of them; at other times he'd turn to me, not speaking, but looking at me with pleading eyes that asked for help and then I would answer for him. The tasks the doctor asked him to complete were clearly impossible. He was unable to write his name and address, and physical tests indicated that his coordination and walking were unreliable. By the end of the appointment the doctors gave a terrifying diagnosis: Simon had classic symptoms of Parkinson's disease, and may have had them for some time. For instance, his expressionless face – which I had found increasingly disturbing and frightening – was a feature of Parkinson's known as "mask face". The doctor said that, with the right medication, some people can live reasonably well. However, determining which drugs are likely to be effective can be difficult to get right—therefore, it would be trial and error to start with. Simon seemed relieved that what was wrong with him had a name, and that medication was on the way. I was shaken, but not shocked. I had been Googling Simon's symptoms for weeks, and knew that this was the likely diagnosis. I had just hoped with all my might that it wouldn't be. We got back to the car and found Winston sound asleep, snoring and warm as toast, thank goodness. We assured each other it was best to know what we were dealing with, and that we'd find the right medication and go for it.

* * *

Throughout the following weeks we battled with the side effects caused by the medication, mainly fatigue and needing to sleep. Simon struggled to stay awake after 1pm each day. Along with increasing tremors, forgetfulness and a general inability to move about, he'd fallen twice and not remembered it happening. Overall, the condition was eating into him. The frozen episodes became more frequent, as did the inability to manage eating. I'd researched cutlery aids as well as other implements to make his life easier, but he flatly refused to use them. He was embarrassed by not being able to feed himself and meals became nightmarish. It would take him 45 minutes to eat a bowl of soup. It pained me, feeling his shame as he'd misjudge his mouth and the food would fall all over him.

Once our GP received Simon's diagnosis, National Health Scotland were onto us and, to this day, I thank God for them. The Parkinson's team in Dumfries were available by phone on a daily basis, training me on how to deal with being the sole carer of a person living with Parkinson's. Their guidance was invaluable, as things with Simon changed constantly, and I needed to keep abreast of what to do. Due to our vulnerable situation, living miles from help and having no support system, our situation was precarious. Though the NHS team was concerned for me, Covid rules and restrictions had tied their hands. They could offer no physical help, only phone guidance. Had we not been so isolated and in lockdown things would have been less frightening but, like the rest of the world, we were stuck at home. I'd researched a basic exercise Parkinson's programme, which we utilised for a short time each day, working on coordination and mind games.

Once again, my beloved ballet community came through for me. Tamara Rojo, a former ballerina who was, at the time, Artistic Director of English National Ballet, put me onto to their Parkinson's Programme leader, and Scottish Ballet followed suit. Immediately we were introduced to their tailor-made Parkinson's internet exercise classes. Simon did his best, but it quickly became clear he was unable to concentrate long enough to continue. The medication was taking its toll: dizziness, confusion and limb tremors escalated in spite of constant adjustments to his prescription. For me, keeping an eye on Simon's safety, making endless food lists and driving twice a week into Castle Douglas for food took strict organisation. I hated leaving Simon alone in the house, as I feared he might fall or walk outside onto the ice and forget how to get back in. I'd be frantic as I queued at Tesco's, clad in winter togs and mask and socially distancing while waiting to get into stores for the following few days' supplies, all the while hoping to God Simon would be safe and warm by the time I returned home.

I updated Simon's family on a regular basis as agreed from the first day of his diagnosis. I'd report every change of medication, mood swing, decline or the rare small improvement. My own education was mounting as I learned to read the signs of oncoming symptoms. Thanks to the support and advice of my NHS counsellors we felt positive that, once the medication had levelled out, we'd be able to find a way to live with this condition.

***

I had confided in only two of my close friends, Margaret Mercer in Perth and Jeanetta Laurence in London. I did not know what to say to our larger circle of friends. Lockdown had put us, like so many others, in a state of uncertainty and fear. Isolation was imperative for us, as we were in the most vulnerable group due to our age and my neutropenia (low white blood cell count), which had been diagnosed some years earlier and increased our need for confinement.

Jeanetta and Margaret dealt with my ranting during long phone calls at odd times. I was losing my beautiful Simon and clinging to moments when he'd be present, holding me and looking at me with his warm, knowing eyes. But these precious moments were fading. I was desperate not to let go of him. On days when Simon was feeling together enough, he would appear to enjoy conversations with family and friends until he ran out of concentration and brought the conversation quickly to an end. Weather permitting, I'd take us out in the car with a thermos of coffee, and little puppy Winston snug in a rug on Simon's knee beside me. Those were lovely moments. Just the three of us.

I had never met anyone in as much need of love as Simon. During rare moments when he would become lucid, we'd talk and plan how we were going to manage living with Parkinson's. No problem, I'd tell him, we'll make it work. Yet it was during these talks Simon would become fearful, afraid things would get too much for me and I'd flee from him. That fear of abandonment would engender panic and shaking. He'd not forgotten past hurt and remained terrified of it happening again. I did my best to reassure him that we were solid and in love. I would never ever leave his side, I said. Usually, this would calm him, at least momentarily.

Life became erratic. Simon's constant mood changes kept me wary and on the alert, as I never knew what was about to erupt. Still, we were hopeful, bumbling along like others suffering from this horrid condition.

* * *

That winter, Scotland was at its most gloomy, with short, grey days and long, black nights that would descend upon us about 4.30pm each afternoon. We were paused with the rest of the world, locked in our tiny bubble, never knowing when freedom might arrive. As much as we could, we jollied each other along. When things got too much, we'd play Pollyanna's glad game and count our blessings: a toasty warm home, food, music and – most of all – being wrapped up in each other's love.

Occasionally, while caring for Simon, the stress I felt would take the form of impatience. The ensuing fragments of anger I evinced would leave me devastated and regretful. At those times, tolerant, kind and understanding Simon would take me in his arms and soothe my guilt. He knew I was doing my best, and together we were doing okay. Later, my NHS counsellor would remind me that being a full-time caretaker comes with massive responsibility, as well as loneliness, confusion, fear and, above all, exhaustion. It was perfectly normal, I was told, that I was sometimes angry and impatient with Simon, especially in our particular circumstances.

About this time I had reason to thank my guardian angel again when Lucy Carlow, an Australian living in the area, came into my life. Lucy and I had previously chatted, sharing our Aussie similarities. We'd got on well, laughing and sharing ideas. Like Simon and Jason, Lucy didn't fit into the village mindset; she was a global thinker, and I found her easy to relate to. As Simon's condition worsened, Lucy recognised that I was having a hell of a time. Uninvited, she stepped up and became a true soul sister and support to me. Looking back, I see how Simon's illness taught me to appreciate more than ever the value of good human beings; those who do not impose but somehow sense precisely what is needed, and provide it without hesitation, not waiting to be asked.

* * *

Christmas of 2020 was a quiet affair worldwide, with lockdown rules being extended and fear mounting as death tolls rocketed; a situation reminiscent of the AIDS crisis. It was a confusing, frustrating time: breaking social distancing rules engendered costly fines; medical appointments were out of the question. Television ads admonished everyone not to touch or hug others. Every day we were bombarded on the telly with English people bleating about how they longed to be hugged, which I thought was hilarious from a nation of non-huggers! Suddenly all we heard was... oh to be hugged!

For Simon, in addition to increased shuffling and lessened mobility came a worrying symptom he described as heartburn, which soon became permanent, severe pain located below his breastbone. It attacked Simon's body with dogged force and occasioned more upon more for him to deal with. I was still an apprentice with much to learn about caring for a person with Parkinson's, and now this new, ugly demon had reared its head. Simon and I were clear that together we could make a good life, but this new pain was uncompromising in its aggression. Swallowing required concentration, and if he could actually swallow, the pain was unbearable. He was losing weight despite my mixing wet food, protein drinks, ice cream and custards. Still he struggled, and nothing seemed to help. The GP insisted this new symptom was caused by anxiety and heartburn. When violent vomiting arrived with a vengeance Simon was in a living hell and getting smaller and smaller.

I was desperate once again, demanding we somehow get Simon an appointment for an endoscopy. This fucking Covid and lockdown. I was enraged by what was happening to our world. Finally, after extreme insistence, an endoscopy was scheduled at Dumfries Infirmary in two weeks. Those two weeks of waiting were horrifically hard on Simon as pain lashed into him. At last, we arrived the hospital for the procedure, which they allowed me to attend.

Watching Simon's throat and oesophagus on the screen while the doctor desperately sought to get the camera down was heart-wrenching. I knew not to panic; we were in crisis. Somehow, brutal reality brings a halt to my anxiety and never fails to steady my nerves. I'm unclear where this comes from, but knowing I have it gives me strength. Perhaps repeated trauma has taught me to remain dependable when dealing with a catastrophe. I was close enough to the screen to see a white wedge of something blocking the camera probe from going further down Simon's oesophagus. Abruptly, the doctor said the procedure could not continue. Simon was shaky and frail. We got back into the car and drove home, having been told to wait for a diagnosis which, due to lockdown, could take weeks.

Those weeks without an answer were hard on us both. We were in free fall along with thousands of others waiting their turn for appointments and medical results. Hospitals were choked with Covid cases, and our beloved NHS was crumbling under the strain of it. Simon was losing more weight daily, unable to swallow, which made eating even the tiniest morsel impossible. I explored every possible option: baby food, blended this and that, failing every single time. The slightest sip of liquid would come back up immediately, which was distressing to us both and sheer agony for Simon. He'd stand beside the kitchen sink when doing his best to get a small drop of liquid into his mouth. This continued for a further three weeks until Simon was waif-like and, as always, uncomplaining. We were afraid things were beyond improvement, and no one was coming to our aid. Eventually, the results came to us. Simon had oesophageal cancer. He had three months to live. Again: the monster wins. I'd been rehearsed in dealing with dire prognoses. I knew it all too well. But I could not accept that, once more, I was going to lose the man I loved so desperately.

* * *

As Simon's cancer gathered force, with it came a further shift in our relationship as the intimacy we'd cherished watered down. Illness simply gets in the way. Protectiveness and the realisation of the scant and precious time we had left shook us to our bones. When thoughts of resentfulness and anger threatened to burst out of me, brought about by utter exhaustion, all would subside at the sight of Simon, humiliated and frustrated because he was no longer able to write or draw which, for an architect, was heart-wrenching. Having always been an absolute doer for himself and others, now he was needing to ask me to check and fetch and carry every little thing for him, all the while apologising incessantly for being so demanding. Witnessing these things, all I could do was forget my tiredness, stand and get on with it.

Simon was in starvation mode: skin and bone, little left of him. Yet, strangely, he became more alert than he had been since diagnosed with Parkinson's some months before.

Something far greater and unstoppable had taken over his life. Weak and ever more frail, he never succumbed and never played the victim. During this time he became emotionally protective of me, tucking me under his wing with all the might he had left. He knew I'd walked this road before and felt blameworthy for putting me through another "death walk" (those were his words, not mine). Did knowing what lay ahead help me? I believe it did. I was in a state of anticipated grief for the end of our life together. Unlike David and Michael's deaths I did not count down the days we had left but concentrated solely on every day as it presented.

A small number of devoted friends stayed in close contact by phone, their warmth and patience supporting us both. One of them, Ricki Gail Conway, would call from her home in New York City. Ricki's husband had late-stage Parkinson's, which they'd be living with for some years. On hearing about Simon's condition, Ricki warned of the strength I was going to need as the disease progressed. I was grateful for her wise advice and constant support throughout those months. Her phone calls frequently pulled me out of a sense that our world was crashing down around us. Her advice came from a place of experience and love. I depended on her straight-talking guidance and took courage from her stoicism. Ricki never pushed or imposed. She simply took my hand.

One freezing cold day I could no longer escape the fact that our situation had become treacherous. Living in lockdown, far from emergency help, we were no longer safe at the house. Simon needed more help than I could provide, and I needed to get him to safety. I bundled him into the car. The night was pitch black, with thick ice covering the country roads. I was fearful as I drove, forging on through the darkness, finally arriving at the Dumfries & Galloway Infirmary. The car park was empty and bleak, not a soul about. We got to the hospital's closed door, rang the emergency bell, and stood there, bitterly cold, as we waited for someone to open the door. Finally, someone answered and ushered Simon into the hospital and led him down a hall. Rigid Covid restrictions meant I could not follow. All I could think was: will I ever see my brave, loving Simon again?

Once back at the house my throat cracked wide open, spewing out the worst-sounding, painful howls. Covid was tearing our world and everyone else's world apart. I remember screaming, "This shitting Covid!!" over and over again. The next few days I spent calling the hospital repeatedly, only to be told that Simon was being taken care of and that no, I could not visit. Knowing there were others, worldwide, in my situation was a thought that periodically eased my furious sense of unfairness.

One morning, I heard a car come up the driveway. This was unusual, as no one ever came to the house. I peeped through the glass door to see a masked Lucy Carlow leaving a basket of food on the doorstep. During the following weeks she would do this again and again. Lucy will never know the pleasure her food gifts bought to me. I had lost weight; I felt frail and spiky. I'd not thought about food for myself in weeks, snatching snacks as they presented. Now, fruit, nuts, home-cooked meals filled my freezer. I remember feeling my body go into overdrive at the thought of nourishing food. Like starving dogs I'd seen in the street, there I was, gobbling every morsel into my aching body. Food had never tasted or felt so good, immediately providing overdue nourishment and helping to appease my raging angst. These days, when asked what's best to take a person in grief or despair, I say "food"; it's the comfort one needs in times of trauma, and the last thing on a traumatised person's agenda. Lucy's baskets of food allowed me to take a mental breather and reassess what was happening. As our friendship developed, I affectionately dubbed her my "Red Riding Hood".

Four days after Simon entered the hospital I received a call saying I could visit him. They'd taken into account my sole caring situation and would allow me into the hospital to visit each day. I will never forget the following few days driving to and from the hospital, grateful that, against all odds, we'd been granted extra time together. I'd arrive back at the house late at night and wash Simon's t-shirts so I could take clean ones to him the following day. Simon, with his sense of style that I adored, hated wearing the hospital gown, preferring to remain elegant even during periods of extreme pain. For a few hours each day in the hospital we'd hold onto each other. I'd stroke his head. He had lost his hair by then, which had been a horrid blow to him. I would tell him how much I loved his bald head at which point he'd smile and tell me how good that made him feel.

On my first day at the hospital, I unexpectedly roller-coastered into a state of panic. We'd been living in isolation for such a long time; suddenly I felt disoriented and scared. Finding myself locked in a confined space surrounded by masked doctors, nurses, cleaners and patients, I thought, *what the hell am I doing besieged at such close proximity by potentially Covid-infected human beings?* I knew that dashing away was not an option. I needed to get a grip on my emotions. I was on a runaway train.

A few days later, Simon's medical team called an around-the-bed meeting with Simon and me. We decided to include Simon's son Robin on the phone so that his family would be up to speed with our next move. There were four members of staff present, explaining the hospital had done all they could for Simon and were recommending, with encouraging words, that the Alexandra Hospice located in the same building could provide Simon with better, specialised care and comfort. Simon, wide-eyed and silent, absorbed their every word. After guiding us carefully through the next stage of hospice care the team leader asked Simon if there was anything he'd like to add to the conversation. After a long pause Simon slowly turned his head to me said, "I want to marry this beautiful woman."

Without taking a breath I replied, "Yes, Simon darling."

Tears flowed from the team; they said they would do all that was necessary to make our marriage happen.

I had no idea how on earth a marriage could be arranged in the short space of time we had left, even as I felt an overpowering feeling of love and contentment which has never abated. We both knew we had no future life together, but it was Simon's way of saying to those who doubted our love *my love for this woman is unending*. This was something he had told me many times. Now he added that he wanted to protect me from what he knew lay ahead. After the medical team left, Simon and I talked about our first meeting in York and how he'd told me with absolute certainty that he was in love with me. That day had been the first time he said his love would be unending... he just knew. Even then.

* * *

That evening, I returned to the house to be met by Jason, who'd popped by to see how Simon was doing. I blurted out that Simon had proposed to me, but I doubted our marriage could happen as time is required to apply for a marriage certificate—time we did not have. Without hesitation, Jason said, "Leave it to me. I will have the documentation here tomorrow night for you to sign and the priest arranged." He had recently married a lovely woman named Kirsty, so was well-versed in the drill. In addition, Simon's palliative doctor, Dr Miller, had gotten an urgent letter to the registrar explaining the gravity of Simon's health and the limited life span we had left together. The following evening, Jason and Kirsty were at the house, papers in hand.

That night I stayed until very late with Simon. The journey back to the house was hazardous. Pitch black, single-lane country roads, icy conditions, no streetlights or other cars. I was exhausted, but there were no options; I had to push on. At the halfway point my phone rang. It was Dr Miller calling from the hospice. I pulled over, switched the car off and listened to his words. He wanted me to know he'd just seen Simon and we were not talking a matter of months left for Simon to live. It could be a few weeks or less. I asked if Simon was going to die that night. Dr Miller assured me he doubted that very much, but that our time was sorely limited.

I made up my mind there and then that I would not leave Simon's side for the time we had left. My reserve strength clocked in instantly, giving me the energy I needed to see this day to its end. I called Lucy Carlow, who instructed me to drive to her home, which was halfway between the hospice and Simon's house, as I was in no condition to drive further. Her partner Brian would drive me the rest of the way. I'd collect little Winston, who'd learnt to stay by himself while I was at the hospital, grab a few essential items and drive me back to the hospice, taking Winston to Lucy. I was blessed to have the support and help of Lucy and Brian that night.

We finally arrived at the hospice well after midnight. I was taken to Simon's room, where the staff had set up a bed beside Simon for me. There I stayed for the following six days. In spite of Covid rules being strictly abided to by way of masks, distancing, every piece of furniture repeatedly wiped, I almost forgot the danger I was living in. While the possibility of my catching Covid in that situation had initially engulfed my being, something far greater had entered my mind. I was free from Covid fear… it had vanished.

Simon was exhausted but relatively pain free thanks to the palliative nurses, who watched over us day and night. The kindness, gentleness and care the palliative team bestowed upon Simon and me was inspirational, and something we desperately needed. We slept in each other's arms and, when awake, lay there together as I reminisced, recalling our relationship from the start: our holidays, long phone calls, emails, longing for each other, my moving up to Scotland, fun weekends in London, all the while bundled into each other.

Three days later, our wedding took place in Simon's room. Simon typically wanted to dress smartly for the service. We were happy as I sorted our outfits, sharing more treasured private moments along the way. Simon asked to wear his special navy jacket we'd bought together in London the previous spring. When, at the very last minute, he asked for his watch we both laughed. I wore a tight red dress that Simon had named my "slinky dress", and threw on some long-forgotten make up. The staff had decorated the room with fairy lights and candles. Kirsty made beautiful flower arrangements and Britt Tajet-Foxell and her partner Peter sent celebratory pink champagne, a tipple that had been the special treat the four of us had revelled in sharing.

Our priest was Reverend Christopher Ketley from St Ninian's Church in Castle Douglas. By chance, he had met Simon a few years before, when he was considering a home renovation. The Reverend is truly kind and thoughtful, and was eager to work with the hospice on our traditional marriage service while keeping within strict Covid rules. Only five people were allowed to attend including Simon, me and our priest. The other two were Jason and Kirsty, who served as our loving witnesses.

The sacred service was conducted in front of a beautifully arranged, small, candlelit altar the staff put together and embellished with flowers and a crucifix. As we made our vows Simon and I wept, as did Kirsty, Jason and our priest. It was a day I will never, ever forget. And I will be forever grateful for the determination and persistence of Jason and Kirsty and Dr Miller, who'd requested that the registrar grant our marriage certificate swiftly. Without them, we could never have achieved our loving marriage. Because of them, Simon got his wish.

* * *

During the next three days, Simon continued to communicate with me by squeezing my fingers each time he heard my loving words. Our intimacy during those days became our last precious, private journey, shared with no other. Off we'd go, whispering words of love known only to us. I have those words locked away inside my head, on call whenever I need to remember my darling Simon. The hospice care allowed us uninterrupted, precious time together, which otherwise we'd not have had. We knew Simon would soon be leaving me forever, and we were grateful to the caring nurses for giving us that last fragment of time.

During the last hours of Simon's life, he became agitated as water seeped into his exhausted lungs, which had worked tirelessly to keep him going over the past few days and hours. Finally, they had run their course, allowing Simon to fade into a place of peacefulness. He continued to squeeze my fingers when I whispered to him but gradually the squeezes became softer and softer. He seemed relieved to be letting go of the struggle to keep breathing. I held onto him, lying beside him, continuing to tell him how much his love had done for me over the past five years when we were cosy and warm and wholly together. Gently, Simon's breathing slowed down. He let go of my fingers and I knew he'd moved away from me. I lay holding him for a long time just to be certain he was at peace. Twenty minutes later, I called his family to let them know Simon had died. We had not had the three months the diagnosis had promised. We had three weeks.

That terrible night, I drove back to the house and spent the night cuddling our little puppy, Winston. Simon's death sent me tumbling into gut-wrenching sadness. I felt I'd been played the meanest of tricks. So many times, I'd thanked God for him and realised the absolute miracle of finding this kind, loving man so late in my life… and then he was gone. How, I wondered, could I survive this all-too-familiar hurt again? Wasn't twice enough? Did I have enough strength left to move through this once more? Honestly, I did not know.

* * *

Simon's funeral was a grim affair. Due to Covid restrictions, only thirty people were permitted in the crematorium. Kirsty, Jason, Lucy and Brian were beside me; the rest were Simon's family and close friends. My previous funeral experience guided me, on automatic pilot, through the necessary motions.

Winston and I stayed at the house for the following seven weeks, after which we would be leaving The Houl for good. Early on in our relationship, Simon and I had drawn up our wills, and I had declined to be a beneficiary. Simon had built the house for himself and his late wife in retirement – a place they could spend time with family and grandchildren – so it felt right that he honour that intention and bequeath the house to them.

Being alone with Winston at The Houl was time I badly needed. Sometimes we slept most of the day, picking at food delivered by life-saver Lucy Carlow. I felt certain that I would know when it was time for us to head down to London, but that seemed a long way off. I had many things to tie up for Simon's estate, and I simply did not have the emotional or physical strength to plan our move. For now, just getting out of bed sapped me of every bit of energy I had left.

To be truthful I can't remember much about those first weeks without Simon. I do recall meandering around the house and spending days gazing across the beautiful landscape that Simon had so carefully chosen for the place to build his home. And so we sat, Winston by my side, his knowing little face slightly perplexed and never missing a single tear that would appear on my cheek. My niece in Australia phoned constantly, and her support was a great comfort.

Little Winston occupied a good deal of my time, walking him, or napping together, or simply curled up on the sofa. He became my need to: I needed to feed him, tend to him, and comfort him. He was missing Simon. The morning I arrived back from the hospice without Simon, Winston had sat at the front door, looking at the car and howling. This went on three days after, when he would sit by Simon's chair looking over at me. We had been a tight threesome, working through Simon's Parkinson's, followed closely by his galloping cancer. Isolation and lockdown had strengthened our bond as we relied on each other for support and love. Winston had lived through Simon's difficult final weeks, never failing to know when to jump up onto his lap and nuzzle up to him. His presence had calmed Simon's anxiety and shaking.

During that time, I never felt isolated or shaky. The solitude was essential, as it provided hours and days in which to gather my thoughts or spew them out. Winston and I were living in Simon's space; he was everywhere. Every inch of the house was taken up with his ideas, his style, his special knack for creating a peaceful and calm space in which to retreat. Yet, even in Simon's lovely haven, I lived in dread of experiencing once again that ravenous grief that had consumed me for so long after David's death. There were desolate days during which I felt desperate to avoid a repeat of that hell.

As the weeks passed, I sensed myself letting go of the home that had provided Winston and me with warmth and comfort. Tears were never far away as I slowly began to pack, asking myself *did this really happen to us?* The answer would immediately follow: Simon was never coming back, so Winston and I needed to go.

* * *

Lucy took me to Dumfries station. I boarded the train as tears streamed down my face. How could it be that arriving at this little station had once filled me with anticipation and longing to be in Simon's arms, knowing the private pleasure we would share was only moments away?

The train journey to London was hazy. I honestly don't remember much about it. What I do recall is gazing out the window pondering, and thinking warm thoughts of Simon. He was a teacher of how to live a life; he led by example, no judging or grandstanding or the need to convince anyone of his cleverness. He was quite simply the most authentic person I've ever loved. Today, as I write, fragments of his likes and dislikes come to mind. I remember, during the first days of our relationship, I called him darling; he looked surprised and told me no one had ever called him darling before. That made me sad. I continued to call him darling till he died. He told me he loved the way I said it.

* * *

London was still in lockdown, which felt odd. I'd never known the city to be so desolate. Where were all the people? But our London flat was warm and welcoming as it had been when I arrived there after David's death. This time my sadness was different. After David and Michael's deaths I'd

224

had the support of so many friends who had cared about both men, and I'd had a global ballet family to share my grief. This time my London set had only met Simon once or twice. I was feeling the weight of aloneness. Perhaps grief is easier if you can connect with others who loved the deceased. And yet, during the hardest times, I did have the support of my family in Australia and my closest, inner circle of friends, who were never far away. I was grateful for their patience, which they seemed to have in abundance. And, once again, Jason and Kirsty came to my rescue, driving from Scotland to deliver my suitcases. How much I appreciated their friendship and encouragement they will never know. I thank God for the care they bestowed upon me.

Puppy Winston arrived by courier from Scotland the day after my arrival. He was excited to see me and soon got used to our tiny flat. Being a Covid pup he'd not been socialised; he'd known only Simon, me, sheep and meadows. What would he make of city life? I decided to jump in right away, so for two weeks we walked the streets of London. Nothing phased him. Ambulances, fire engines, police cars, trucks— he took it all in his stride. As long as we were together, he was totally cool. His kind and loyal breeder, Jill Allitt, graciously offered to take him back, refunding our money should he not settle in. Jill knew there were no thoughts in my mind of returning him, but she was concerned, knowing the journey Winston and I had travelled. Her support has been ongoing regarding Winston's upbringing and she has become a solid friend.

* * *

My announcement that Simon and I had married, followed days later by Simon's death, had caused understandable confusion. My London friends tried to piece together this jumbled news, which I was in no state to clarify. Unexpectedly, a dear friend in New York, Sian Burman, who had been a highly respected dancer in The Australian Ballet, saw what was happening on social media and acted as a rescue service, detailing the situation, and relieving me of explanation.

Over the next weeks, I was reminded of the love and care that comes so easily to many human beings, those who know when urgency strikes not to wait for permission to respond. They were my guardian angels, who reached out, offering help. Nothing was too much trouble; they knew I was trapped in a tsunami that was not readily going to subside. Then there were those who forgave my blunders or overtired, sharp reactions and didn't judge or reprimand, but spoke with empathy and allowed me to make amends when some measure of healing had tiptoed in. Yet, despite these many kindnesses, I was struggling. I felt unable to speak my truth. I didn't want to risk exposing to my friends how raw I was feeling in fear that they'd had enough of my sorrow. I tried to uphold my warrior image, never wanting to appear the victim looking for sympathy. But at the same time, hurt devoured me. In that state, well-meant light-heartedness or efforts to soothe my turmoil could render me unhinged. When some friends surprised me with an insensitive or uncaring reply, those moments cut deep. I sought to use them as a reminder not to ask too much of anyone.

I knew if I could spew out my feelings of injustice to the right person, free from judgement and empty words, I could steady myself. So the best I could do, I decided, was find a therapist. I set about Googling therapists in West London, where there were many. This research was a first, small step toward sorting out my life, and it felt good. I selected six therapists who seemed possible and called them all, leaving messages to please call me back, which eventually they did. Only one of the six picked up the phone. Her name was

Kelly Hearn. I was startled that a human being actually answered. Kelly recognised my surprised tone and we chuckled. I briefed her regarding my situation, and she was quick to clock into the yearning I had to improve my life. A date was set for my first session. Instantly I felt my power returning. It was another small step, but one that affirmed that I was taking control of my life. My feeling of spinning out eased up.

Initially, every session provided the exact opportunity I needed to vent my pain and despair. Tears would flow. I'd found what I needed: a safe place to let go of my pent-up hurt and disappointment that Simon had died and taken with him all we'd looked forward to and planned for our champagne years, as we had called them. Now it is ten months later, and I seldom cry. I've been able to talk openly to Kelly about the unfairness of what happened in my life. Verbalising my thinking in private surroundings where I can be free from the fear of judgment has brought relief and allowed me to spend time with friends engaged in our joint interests, rather than burdening them by ruminating on my loss.

During one of my early treatments Kelly asked if I had ever thought of writing about my life, to which I replied in a rather astonished voice "no". She went on to suggest I might think about jotting down my thoughts as a way of finding some clarity. A week later I gingerly jotted down a few random memories, which have become the book you are reading. Once I started writing, my computer was never closed. I liken the experience to being immersed in a ballet or working on a piece of choreography. Ballet is my addiction, and to this day I cannot really explain the sensation it stirs in me, but writing comes very close.

PART FIVE

AND NOW

My journey has been a kaleidoscope of ecstatic love and despair, tumbling me through highs, lows, and everything in between. These days, I'm foraging through my very own amusement arcade of good fortune, successes, heartbreak and tons of laughter, which allows me to while away hours, boosted by treasured memories. I'm grateful for the sheer serendipity from which I've benefitted throughout my life that has brought me the companionship of witty, smart people, not because I'm overly witty or smart myself; I'm simply a good audience and love the challenge of keeping up.

A short time ago, I made a drastic change when I was suddenly drawn to decluttering, lightening my load, and taking on a minimalist way of life. I've never been a collector as such, so the shift was relatively easy. Out went every single thing I was not using. The local charity shop did well. How hilarious to trot by it and see my debris in the window. This transformation was enlightening. I felt free of excess baggage, having created space not only in my surroundings but in my mind. I remember when Simon, having noted the way my belongings were lined up so neat and tidy, asked if I had OCD because he'd never known anyone as meticulous. I responded that I possibly do, and if that were the case it was certainly a good trait to have as a ballet dancer! My declutter plan of action progressed into a full-blown square-away, leave-no-stone-unturned scheme that extended to finalising my will and end-of life-instructions, as I had taken the lesson from my parents not to leave a wretched mess for others – in this case my niece and nephew – to clean up.

From repeated experience I know that, once terminal illness strikes, even the best hospice palliative care cannot guarantee a peaceful death. Some conditions come with pain so extreme it is beyond controlling. Without doubt, should I be diagnosed with a lingering terminal condition I will take control of my end of life. This decision has strengthened my sense of freedom, allowing me to feel at leisure with the champagne years I have left. Close friends and my niece and nephew acknowledge my decision respectfully, knowing it arrives from careful thought and familiarity with the end of human life.

When I look back now, I can appreciate why it was that finding myself in the position of caring for another human being's life came with confusion, exhaustion, and feelings of fear and powerlessness over what I knew lay ahead. Was it all too hard, too big an ask? At times undoubtedly yes—but ultimately it was neither too hard nor too big, because my caring for Michael, David and Simon came from a place of love.

Hospice nursing provided care and support as well easing the insurmountable fatigue that accumulates when taking care of a terminally ill person. Fear of how death will present can be a daunting thought, and step-by-step guidance on what to expect before and during the last moments is helpful. At each hospice, the staff shared my pain and were there with support when fear, despair and powerlessness crashed in. Spending considerable time in hospices acquainted me with our cultural differences in dealing with the sacred rite of dying. Some cultures gather the entire community: family, extended friends and elders stand by, waiting, linked in love and support. I also noticed that in other cultures, people flee when death is clearly imminent, leaving their loved one alone, waiting for God.

In my experience, hospice care was, in almost every case, positive. However, I take into account that my presence was constant, 24 hours a day, always alert, on guard and ready to spring into action, calling for help whenever needed. I would be saddened if the staff ever felt I was scrutinising their work or judging their care. With the sole exception of David being denied the pain medicine he required, I had no time for such notice. My concern was fixated on the person in the bed, whom I loved. When my dearest loves were fading and near to death, the gift we needed most was time. Time for each other. Time to whisper, hold, stroke, explain, cry, or apologise. Privacy and space permits love to flow, and sometimes you can forget, even for one precious moment, that the end is near.

* * *

Sixteen months after Simon died, I went to my beloved Greek island Hydra. I wondered, *how will I feel*? I'd rehearsed for this many times. I knew what to expect and how to prepare myself. Leaving little Winston was made softer by the kindness of my long-time, good friends Rashna and Stephen Jefferies, who offered to look after him while I was away. Leaving him was a big decision for me, but Rashna and Stephen know what this little dog means to me, and I felt blessed to know he would be loved and safe.

When I arrived at the little port, everything looked the same. Donkeys overloaded with cases, shuttered doors, cobblestone pathways uneven and hot, brown bodies draped in cotton sarongs, cats of all description and the relentless, searing heat. Locals thrust a welcome wave as I trudged from the JetCat to the Bratsera Hotel. Released from the London threat of cars, bikes and scooters, Hydra offered gentleness, a sense of *take your time no one's going to bulldoze you.*

Wispy wind, lapping of waves against the rocks and the absence of vehicles had always brought me serenity.

Room 11, my cool nest at the end of the garden away from the other residents, awaited my arrival, shutters drawn. The key to my room, as always, was a heavy monster of a thing; finally, it worked, and I was facing the large red tapestry on the wall over the bed—a beautiful reminder of ancient Greek and Turkish embroidery.

I knew that, by taking this trip, I was attempting to bridge the 50-year span since I first fell in love with the island. But, with so much time having passed, I inevitably noticed differences: unpacking felt strangely complicated, and I struggled to sort my small case of clothing and books. I felt at a crossroad: tired, exhausted. Unstoppable tears cascaded down my face. I was in a tattered state, threadbare for how long I cannot remember. Eventually I surfaced, searching for my reliable, defiant courage. Support arrived by way of words from therapist Kelly in London, reminding me that my anguish and pain is the flip side of deep love.

The heat and humidity of Hydra took my breath away. I stayed cosseted in my room for four days, emerging only for a morsel of food in the hotel restaurant. I was comforted by the familiarity of my surroundings but, again, I felt the change in me. I was less agile, the sturdiness my body once had was absent. I tiptoed outside, buffeted by the hot wind and relentless, punishing heat. I scuttled back inside, vulnerable, sad and a little bit angry. I had booked to spend two weeks on the island but cut it short by one week. I had wanted to feel the love hormone Hydra always evoked in me, but it had gone.

* * *

In October 2022, two months after my trip to Hydra, I received word from Australia that my nephew's partner had suddenly died. She was 56. Having lost his beloved, Benson was desolate and, since I am the oldest living relative in our family, my instinct was to be with him. So I made the journey to Australia. There, I looked on as harsh waves of grief thrashed my nephew. There were no adequate words. But Benson knew I'd walked in his shoes. My presence carried the weight of experience, and that was enough. Witnessing his level of despair offered a new perspective on how far I had travelled from that harrowing place of sorrow. The misery I had experienced in the wake of Simon's death was feeling softer. I was loosening and sensing more and more the release of that pent-up hurt.

Returning to London I felt richer than when I'd left two weeks before. As I struggled to process this unexpected emotion it struck me that my own loss had found a place of usefulness by offering to my nephew the gift of hope. After that trip, I began to feel the tug of family in Australia; I welcomed being the great-great aunt to the youngest in my clan. And I could see that, somehow, my familiarity with death had diluted a measure of my grief, and that this would allow me to live my life in a way that is bearable.

It's December 2022. Winter is setting in fast. Christmas lights twinkle from Victorian sash windows and London is adorned with a white cape of fresh snow. I imagine the Snow Queen whooshing past, en route to her ice palace. A moment of dreaming is welcome, time out from those unexpected moments of grief that still stubbornly lurk and pounce. There are no templates or instructions on how to navigate the turbulence when it buffets me around.

I see now that dealing with adult issues during my childhood and managing my life from a young age was preparation for the challenges life was going to throw at me. I always knew that Michael, David and Simon were capable of breaking my spirit—and they did when they left, taking a part of me with them. Yet, increasingly, I've experienced an ease about living without their physical presence, though what never leaves my being is the sensation of their tenderness. And that keeps me upright and comforted. Today, I have time to look back and indulge in longing for the men I lost, and although those memories induce moments of sorrow, they are also precious and sweet. Until recently I was not aware of how easily the names of Michael, David and Simon filter through my conversation. The fact is, speaking their names brings warmth to my skin and provides a reminder of how lovingly I've been touched.

And then I ask myself, would I risk falling in love again at 77? Yes indeed. The fondness that comes with love would be impossible to resist. I live best when I'm in love. But, regardless of what happens or doesn't happen in the future, I'm grateful for the abundance of love I've had. And I know that only when I was able to let go of grief was it possible for me to love again. I'm also grateful to have lived this long in relatively good health. Many have not been so fortunate. I hope in my coming years to be a better playfellow. These days, I keep my cosmetic purse close at hand, believing a dash of red lipstick shows I can scrub up okay at any given moment! And how lucky I am to have my devoted dog, Winston, who is more knowing than most people. After all, he's witnessed me at my most broken and understood exactly when to snug into my arms and rest his head on my shoulder. He listens politely to my grunts as I manoeuvre my way across the sofa protecting my back from jarring. He then collects his lead as if saying "Get up! Let's go!" Not so long ago I referred to Winston as my crying pillow. But not anymore.

***

May 2023. Sunshine at last. London finally bidding farewell to her endless gloom. Wisteria and croci sprout, eager to welcome the warmth of summer. For just a few lovely weeks London will adopt her best face, encouraging us to escape from our dark homes with drawn drapes and inefficient heating. I'm feeling hopeful, though slightly wistful, knowing that summers on my beloved Hydra have run their course. Most significantly, I've made the decision to return to my roots in Australia. Family, relentless sunshine, hot, balmy nights, warm sand under my feet... time to go.

I'm on a roll already, flirting with packing; not that there's much to pack, thanks to my minimalist style. How exquisitely small my world has become, occupied mostly by Winston, family, a few dear friends and treasured memories. My lifelong love of art in all forms, especially ballet, will travel with me; we've never been separated, not ever. Each time my world fell apart – which as you know it had a habit of doing – my salvation was music and dance. It was there for me, underpinning my life, supporting me through treacherous times.

What a remarkable 59-year journey I was gifted. No wonder I'm feeling full-up and ready to head back to my homeland *alone*, exactly as I left all those years ago. David will rejoice at my returning to his beloved Australia. I will place his ashes under the willow tree, just as he asked. Recently, having sorted my end of life. I've become determined to remain useful, and I'm gratified that the Anatomical Society has agreed to accept my ballet bones. I twinkle just a tiny bit at the thought that maybe a young medical student will wonder what this old lady contributed to the world.

As I write this, it is eight weeks from the 14th year since David's death. I know this because the tempting June sunlight is tinged with a spiky, cold wind—that same wind that sent David and I scurrying inside, away from the lovely garden at the hospice. The peonies are blooming, alerting me to the date and time, forever beautiful and accurate in their reminder.

Should you arrive at the place I did, faced with losing the person you most love, perhaps, like me, you will take strength from the intimacy, privilege and sacredness of being with them and holding onto them during that final journey. As for myself, I believe I've learnt something important from seeing first-hand when a life has run its course. Now that my own time is running out, I will continue to adhere to the mantra I adopted years ago: *Get Up, Dress Up, Show Up*. Beyond that, I intend to do the sensible thing and fill whatever time remains with as much love and fun as I can.

Having already had a lifetime of love, I will not complain.

AFTERWORD AND ACKNOWLEDGEMENTS

Initially writing was, for me, a form of therapy—a simple act of quieting the continual monkey chatter in my head. The seclusion that accompanies the lengthy business of writing is something I thoroughly enjoy, and I found myself looking forward to opening my computer each day. My memory is sharper than I'd dared imagine, and the more I wrote the more I dreaded the day THE END would appear in print.

Throughout this process I've been supported by a small group of unique and inspirational women whose opinions I hold in high esteem. Their persistence and dogged belief in my story fuelled me and gave me the energy I needed to plough ahead. They are:

Rachel Hollings, my dearly loved friend, whose ingenious instinct and long-sightedness envisioned a creative coupling between myself and Elizabeth Kaye who, at her suggestion, would become my Los Angeles-based editor. Rachel's love, knowledge and infectious wit kept me on track and supported me throughout. I'd never have made it to THE END without her passion and belief in my story. I knew I was blessed when, many years ago, our special relationship was bestowed upon me and became a treasure I cherish. Her steadfastness has always been at the ready to reignite my energy or tame my impatience.

Elizabeth Kaye, my editor, who affirmed my need to write. The one who guided my hand as I dug into the crevices of my life, enabling me to find a purpose for so much loss.

Permanently beside me while I navigated burningly cruel truths that had to be written. Her acute intelligence and innate love of language allowed her to translate my every thought with remarkable tenderness. Her in-depth knowledge and love of ballet enmeshed us in a partnership that allowed this endeavour to flourish. I could never have taken the journey of writing without her guidance and love.

Kelly Hearn, my therapist. The first to read my anguished writing; the woman whose eyes widened as she read the first words I wrote. She was the one who told me, "Petal you have a story to tell: keep writing." And later, the memorable day when she referred to my text as "the book". Those two words were the beginning of sunlight returning to my life. Knowing my worst fears, longings and tears were safe with Kelly allowed me to soothe my broken heart and commence healing.

Sally Phoenix, whose creative conversation nourished my thoughts, providing the courage I needed to write my truth. Her enthusiasm as I began this book provoked my need to reminisce, explore my past, and write.

Carina Sas, my niece, whose fine and sensitive mind never failed to inspire. The first to suggest long ago that her aunt had a story to be shared by way of writing. Gifted with ideas and perceptiveness in abundance, she was always reliably generous with considered feedback.

Rachel Thomas, who gathered the finale of this book, and whose gracious spirit, sincere effort and eagle eye guided me to The End.

The care and love these women bestowed upon me throughout this journey is permanently stored in my heart.

Special thanks to **Maggie's, Dignity in Dying** and the **Terrence Higgins Trust** for their invaluable support and hope at some of the most difficult times in my life. Caring for a terminally ill human being is living in a state of alertness, with the looming threat of emergency never far away. Often it is the carer who pacifies the night terrors and holds steadfast again and again during the very worst life has to offer. Unspoken, the resulting grief can be shattering – causing a person to run for cover and recoil into aloneness – and organisations such as these that helped me play a vital role in giving grief a voice, allowing it to be heard and honoured not silenced.

And finally, a word to **Michael, David** and **Simon:** when beavering away on this text it so often seemed I was talking to you. The three of you have been my most ardent lovers and caretakers of my deepest thoughts and desires. You will not read this book, but I must tell you... I will love you forever.

For you, the reader, it is my hope that what I have written in these pages will allow you to reach a deeper understanding of loss, its complex aftermath, and the need to find a way forward. And, if you have experienced a loss similar to mine, perhaps my story will leave you feeling less alone. Should something embedded in my words bring you even the smallest measure of hope and comfort, I will be happy.

P

REFLECTIONS, PROGRESS
AND HOPE FOR THE FUTURE

An early note from my editor:

*You've endured the sort of loss every human dreads, yet
your grace and verve is evidence of the fact that such
losses can be borne, and that we go on because we must
and make the most of our days, our own existence.*

That's a huge story Petal – an important one.

Elizabeth Kaye

You will have read that Dr Mike Youle was Michael's doctor.
I asked him how far medicine had come with treating AIDS.
This is what he wrote:

*AIDS in the 1980s was brutal, and we could offer little
to those getting sicker with HIV except to ease their
symptoms and give them dignity in death. Michael
was one of many who did not live to see the future of
effective treatment, which is now usually one pill daily
with few side effects and the promise of a normal,
healthy life span. The change in care for HIV since then
has been seismic, and it now represents an easily treated,
though sadly still a markedly stigmatised condition.*

*I remember Michael as constantly smiling—in his house
with its rooftop hideaway in Islington, lounging on a deck
on Fire Island and showing me how to really dance at a
Leather and Rubber Ball in Brixton Town Hall. I have
fond memories and great photographs of us together. I
wish he was still here to reminisce about those happy times.*

Dr Mike Youle

PHOTOGRAPHS

Milton Keynes UK
Ingram Content Group UK Ltd.
UKHW011139220424
441551UK00007B/670